PRAISE FOR
WE NEED TO TALK

"This book is necessary. . . . Headlee's treatise on creating space for valuable mutual reciprocity is one that should become a handbook in any school, business, or even a doctor's office where the everyday person visits." —George Elerick, *Buzzfeed*

"In the course of her career, Headlee has interviewed thousands of people from all walks of life and learned that sparking a great conversation is really a matter of a few simple habits that anyone can learn." —Jessica Stillman, *Inc.*

"Refreshingly honest. . . . In the era of the lost art of conversation, Headlee helps us find our voice." —Patrik Henry Bass, *Essence*

"Civil discourse is one of humanity's founding institutions and it faces an existential threat: we, the people, need to talk about how we talk to one another. Celeste Headlee shows us how." —Ron Fournier, *New York Times* bestselling author of *Love That Boy* and publisher of *Crain's Detroit*

WE NEED
TO TALK

WE NEED TO TALK

HOW TO HAVE CONVERSATIONS THAT MATTER

CELESTE HEADLEE

HARPER WAVE

An Imprint of HarperCollins*Publishers*

A hardcover edition of this book was published in 2017 by Harper Wave, an imprint of HarperCollins Publishers.

HarperCollins books may be purchased for educational, business, or sales promotional use. For information, please e-mail the Special Markets Department at SPsales@harpercollins.com.

FIRST HARPER WAVE PAPERBACK EDITION PUBLISHED 2018.

Designed by Leah Carlson-Stanisic

Library of Congress Cataloging-in-Publication Data has been applied for.

ISBN 978-0-06-266901-8 (pbk.)

22   LSC   10

FOR GRANT

I wanted to be a better person so I could be a better mom.

CONTENTS

CONTENTS

INTRODUCTION

On January 13, 1982, a tragedy occurred just outside Washington, DC. More than six inches of snow fell at Ronald Reagan National. The airport was closed for most of the morning and reopened at noon. Air Florida Flight 90 had already been severely delayed when the captain had to make a choice about whether or not to take off. He could wait a little longer and have the plane de-iced one more time, or he could depart immediately and try to get his passengers back on schedule. It had been forty-nine minutes since the plane was de-iced. He chose to take off.

We know from the plane's voice recorder[1] that soon after takeoff, the first officer tried to warn the captain that something was wrong.

FIRST OFFICER: Look how the ice is just hanging on his back there, see that? See all those icicles on the back there and everything?
CAPTAIN: Yeah.

FIRST OFFICER: Boy, this is a losing battle here on trying to de-ice those things; it [gives] you a false feeling of security, that's all that does.

[*Some minutes go by*]

FIRST OFFICER: God, look at that thing, that don't seem right, does it? [*3-second pause*] Ah, that's not right. Well—

CAPTAIN: Yes, it is, there's 80. [Referring to the airspeed]

FIRST OFFICER: Naw, I don't think that's right. [*7-second pause*] Ah, maybe it is . . . I don't know.

What neither pilot realized was that the readings in the cockpit weren't reliable because the instruments were clogged with ice. Also, the captain never turned on the heater in the plane's engines. About thirty-five seconds after the plane left the ground, we have this exchange from the cockpit:

FIRST OFFICER: Larry, we're going down, Larry.

CAPTAIN: I know it.

The plane slammed into the Fourteenth Street Bridge and then plunged into the Potomac River. Seventy-eight people died; only five ultimately survived.

The crash of Air Florida Flight 90 is seen as a pivotal moment in the development of airline safety standards; it prompted the Federal Aviation Administration (FAA) to study how often a plane should be de-iced, how to create longer-lasting de-icing chemicals, and how airplane instruments are affected by cold temperatures. Experts also spent a lot of time studying that exchange in the cockpit, captured by the black box.

Twenty years later, I read about this incident while researching a story and it made me rethink my entire philosophy on conversation. Most communication experts who listened to the black box recording concluded that copilots should be trained to be more direct with their captains. But my first thought when I read the transcript was that we need to train pilots to listen better. I'd never before considered that improving conversational techniques could be a survival skill.

It may seem that the stakes will never be that high for most of us—that lives will never hang in the balance of our conversations. But let me ask you this: have you ever been admitted to a hospital? Oftentimes, lives *are* at stake. Communication failures led to 1,744 deaths[2] in American hospitals between 2009 and 2013, and that includes only the cases that were tracked because a malpractice suit was filed. "Communication failures" is a fairly broad term used to describe everything from a night nurse failing to relay vital information to the nurse working the next shift to a doctor prescribing treatment without reviewing a patient's chart. It also includes breakdowns in communication with patients and their family members, who often arrive at the hospital anxious and confused.

Imagine for a moment how important it is to get these conversations exactly right. The need for brevity and efficiency must be balanced with careful listening. There are any number of emotional factors (physical pain, stress, confusion, anger) that could derail such a conversation and an equal number make it vital that the exchange be clear and comprehensive.

Personally, I'm grateful lives don't hang in the balance when I converse on the radio every day. But important, life-changing events are influenced and affected by the words we choose to say or leave unspoken.

Take a moment to consider how many opportunities you may have missed, how many outcomes in your life may have been altered because of poor communication. Could you have landed that dream job if you'd nailed the interview? Saved a relationship if you'd been more open about certain issues? What about that political conversation at Thanksgiving dinner that got out of hand; was there a different way to defend your principles so that your cousin didn't storm away from the table (and still won't return your text messages)?

After I read the cockpit transcripts from Flight 90, I spent a lot of time reflecting on how many times I've failed to get my point across in a conversation and how often I've misunderstood what someone else was trying to tell me. I've also realized that saying the wrong thing in a conversation is a universal experience. We've all lost something because of what we said or didn't say, what we failed to hear, or what we heard and misunderstood. So we can all benefit from learning a better way.

Some of my greatest insights have come about as the result of failures. And one of my most valuable lessons in listening resulted from my failure to listen. Two days after the massive earthquake in Haiti in 2010, I spoke on air with a woman in Michigan named Mallery Thurlow. She had been trying for two days to reach her fiancé in Port-au-Prince and had been unsuccessful. She was desperate to reach him or anyone else who might be able to tell her if her loved ones were alive or dead.

Our production staff worked tirelessly to track down her fiancé, France Neptune, and we brought them both onto the air. Mallery and France heard each other's voices for the first time since the earthquake[3] and my co-host and I listened as the couple spoke with each other, relief and gratitude audible in every syllable. It was moving for all of us. Up to that point, we were listening to a powerful conversation, but I should have stopped congratulating myself over a well-planned segment and really listened to where the discussion was headed.

We weren't expecting France to inform Mallery on live radio that her young godchild had died in the collapse of a school building. Mallery, not surprisingly, began to cry. I wasn't sure what to say. It was an uncomfortable moment for me and I can only imagine it was painful for the thousands of listeners who felt they were intruding on a highly personal and agonizing conversation. Our station later received a number of complaints.

Even if you set aside the humanity involved, that a person has just learned of the death of a loved one while thousands of people listened in, her tears don't make for a good broadcast. Hearing someone cry on the radio is painful, not powerful. Most people, understandably, want to console the person and can't. They want me, the host, to console the guest, and often I don't have the words or time to do so. If I had been listening more carefully, I would have heard the turn in the conversation. I could have ended the segment and allowed Mallery and France their privacy. I didn't, and it still bothers me. I was too caught up in my own story to pay attention to theirs.

In my private life, I've lost contact with family members and I've seen friendships die in silence when I failed to say what was really on my mind. I've suffered in my career as well because I couldn't seem to make myself understood during important conversations with recruiters or managers.

I now believe that conversation may be one of the most fundamental skills we can learn and improve upon. So much hinges on what may seem like trivial chats. In fact, my entire career in radio began because of a casual conversation.

In 1999, I had just finished my master's degree at the University of Michigan. My fiancé was overseas in Kosovo with the army and I was in Arizona with our infant son. I stopped by KNAU, Arizona Public Radio, because they were recording an interview with my mom about her father.

My grandfather had been a famous composer, often called the dean of African American composers, and an important figure in US history. His list of "firsts" is quite long: the first black man to conduct a major US symphony orchestra, the first to conduct an orchestra in the Deep South, the first to have an opera produced by a major company, and more. My mother is often interviewed about him, and on that occasion I was tagging along.

The music director at KNAU, it turns out, was an old friend. We got to chatting. I don't know what I said but at one point she blurted out, "So! Do you want a job?" She needed a weekend classical music announcer and it's not easy to find qualified candidates. A classical music radio host has to possess a deep knowledge of classical music, along with the ability to pronounce names like Camille Saint-Saëns and Sofia Asgatovna Gubaidulina. I held two degrees in music and not only could I pronounce Johannes Brahms, but I could also tell you juicy stories about his part in a love triangle with Robert and Clara Schumann.

I took the job and the rest is history. I've worked as a local announcer, a reporter, a correspondent, and a host of national shows for National Public Radio and Public Radio International. I've been a featured guest on CNN and the BBC, and I anchored presidential coverage for PBS World. I think it's fair to say I must have done something right along the way. But the moments that stay with me, the ones that sometimes keep me up at night, are those in which I failed to make a connection or failed to make myself understood. Moments when I didn't really hear what someone was telling me or understand that they were asking for help.

There have been some important conversations in

my life, the kinds that probably changed the course of it for good or ill. Did I say what I needed to say? Was I understood? Did I listen to what I was told? How much did I miss? These are the questions that plague me. I can't help but think that they also plague others.

In 2014, when the organizers of TEDx Augusta approached me to speak at their event, they asked me to think about something that really bothered me and then write about how I could change it. There was no question or hesitation in my mind; what bothered me the most were those lost moments. And the more I began to think about them, the more I realized that collectively, as a society, those moments are taking a toll. Our conversational skills have eroded; it seems like we rarely converse anymore. I mean, we talk and we chat (often over text or e-mail), but we don't really hash things out. We spend a lot of time avoiding uncomfortable conversations and not enough time making an effort to understand the people who live and work around us.

It's hard to overestimate the power of conversation. It's hard to say too much about the gaps it can bridge and the wounds it can heal. At its best, conversation is a potent force for good. But when it goes wrong, that force can be equally damaging, equally harmful.

What I've seen in my own country and around the

globe is what happens when conversation goes wrong or doesn't happen at all. And the irony is, we talk *about* conversation all the time. How many calls have there been in the United States for a "national conversation" on drugs, race, law enforcement, education, or immigration? Over and over we say we need to talk about issues and then we proceed to shout out our own opinions with no regard to what the other side is saying. That's not a conversation!

Our world has become so fractured by politics and distracted by technology that having a meaningful conversation about anything has become a challenge. As Wesley Morris wrote in the *New York Times*, "We used to talk, and people would listen. . . . People still gathered for the evening news. Mass culture was experienced *en masse*. A national conversation involved a large portion of the public talking about both important and frivolous stuff more or less at the same time."[4]

It may be that the conversations that matter most won't be held on a national stage at all, but rather in office cubicles or grocery store aisles. It might be that authentic conversations can't happen online but only in living rooms and lunchrooms and airports and restaurants.

No matter how much you like to think of yourself as

a private person, your actions affect those around you in real, tangible ways. Like the famous flutter of Edward Lorenz's butterfly that eventually causes a hurricane, what you do has implications for the wider world around you. We must learn how to talk to one another and, more important, listen to one other. We must learn to talk to people we disagree with, because you can't unfriend everyone in real life.

This book could not be more personal to me. I was asked what bothered me and how I might change it. What bothers me is that we don't talk *to* each other but *at* each other, and we usually don't listen. With this book, I hope to play some small part in changing that.

PART I

Conversation. What is it? A Mystery! It's the art of never seeming bored, of touching everything with interest, of pleasing with trifles, of being fascinating with nothing at all.

—GUY DE MAUPASSANT

1

CONVERSATION IS A SURVIVAL SKILL

E-volve comes from "to roll out." Con-verse comes from "to turn together." We can rightly say that—as we turn together in conversation, we become the evolution we've been waiting for.

—THE CO-INTELLIGENCE INSTITUTE

Nuanced conversation is a uniquely human skill. Biologists think it's a compelling force behind our success as a species and our ascent up the food chain. Although the precise chronology of when humans first started talking is still up for debate, it is safe to say that we've been jabbering coherently for at least a million years.

How has this ability helped us? Well, for one thing, we can lie and other animals can't. When a cat doesn't like you, you know it. A dog can't fake a growl and elephants, so far as we know, can't pretend to grunt. Humans can dissemble and, while that might be seen as a flaw, it's often useful.

For example, imagine you couldn't pretend that you like your mother-in-law or your boss. Imagine you couldn't tell your friend who's had a rough day that her haircut looks great. Imagine you couldn't tell your prospective employer that you planned to stay with the company for at least five years. Lying carries a negative connotation for good reason, but it's also an essential skill. And it's one that only humans have, to the best of our knowledge. (My dogs pretend they haven't been fed in the morning to see if they can coerce a second breakfast out of my son, but I guess science doesn't consider that "lying.")

Conversation has long been a crucial asset to us as a species. Compared to other creatures, physical attributes are not among our strengths. We admire the swiftness of the snow leopard, the poison of the Komodo dragon, or the sheer power of a polar bear. I'm sure we all know that we can't win a hand-to-paw fight with a grizzly bear. We are not at the top of the food chain, of course.[1] On a scale of 1 to 5, we score 2.21. That puts us on a par with anchovies.

And yet, despite all of our physical weaknesses, we are the dominant species. It is perhaps *because* of our comparatively fragile forms that humans have had to find other ways to compete, and talking was one of our most powerful tools. Seth Horowitz, an auditory neuroscientist, says this:

> *We think about ourselves as being the new smartest rulers of the planet, but our ears have evolved, and the basic brain circuitry of hearing has evolved over 400 million years, and a lot of it centered on hearing the sound of your own species. That's the most important signal, even if you can't see them. Hearing evolved as your alarm system, because we're diurnal, we don't see well at night, but our hearing is running all through the darkness and even when we are asleep. A sound, even without a visual tie to it, is very important to us. We've evolved to listen to other people talk.*[2]

Many evolutionary biologists posit that humans developed language for economic reasons. We needed to trade, and we needed to establish trust in order to trade. Language is very handy when you are trying to conduct business with someone. Two early humans could not only agree to trade three wooden bowls for six bunches of bananas but arrange terms as well. What wood was used for the bowls? Where did you get the bananas? That transaction would have been nearly impossible using only gestures and unintelligible noises, and carrying it out according to terms agreed upon creates a bond of trust.

Language allows us to be specific, and this is where conversation plays a key role. Your cat can tell you that he's in pain and in a lot of pain, but he can't tell you what hurts or describe the injury. We can do that, plus rank the pain on a ten-point scale, tell you when it started hurting, and whether it's a shooting pain or more of an ache. That's a powerful survival tool.

Some scientists suggest language evolved as a part of mating. We can observe a similar phenomenon in other species. The ability to make certain sounds and imitate others might make you attractive to a member of the opposite sex. (Although when it comes to human mating, this skill can prove to be a double-edged sword. I'm reminded of Abraham Lincoln's words: *Better to remain silent and be thought a fool than to speak and to remove all doubt.*)

Whatever the original imperative for human speech, we have developed languages that rise far above a dog's warning bark or a snake's intimidating hiss. "We can use our language to look into the future," says evolutionary biologist Mark Pagel, author of *Wired for Culture*. "[We can] share the thoughts of others, and benefit from the wisdom of the past. We can make plans, cut deals, and reach agreements. We can woo prospective mates and threaten our enemies. We can describe who did what to whom, when they did it, and for what reason. We can describe how to do things, and what things to avoid."[3]

In fact, the human body is uniquely evolved for conversation. We started out with the same basic equipment that chimps have: lips, tongue, lungs, throat, soft palate, and larynx. Those tools allow us to make noises.

(Actually, if your goal is just to create sounds and not specific noises, you don't even need a throat, just a balloon. Inflate it and then let the air out slowly while you change the size of the neck. See the thin plastic vibrating at different speeds as you stretch it out or relax it? That's similar to what happens inside your throat. Your vocal cords vibrate as breath passes over them.)

But we needed to make more than noises. And one of the ways we evolved differently from our ape cousins is that we developed the ability to form words. Our mouths shrank while our necks got shorter. Our lips became more flexible. We've even paid a high price for this evolutionary advantage because our larynx eventually moved farther down our throats. We have an additional open space back there called the pharynx. The pharynx is formed of walls of muscle that move food into the esophagus and warm up the air we breathe before it travels to the lungs.

7

These changes to our mouths and necks made it possible for us to form words, but they also meant that food must travel farther, past the larynx to the esophagus, in order to be digested. If it gets stuck along the way and blocks our airway, we choke. Consider that for just a moment: the human race risks death in order to communicate more clearly. That's how crucial language is to our species.

It's important to note that language is not the same as communication. We can communicate in complete silence, using gesture, eye contact, and touch. But language is required for conversation. Although sign language is silent, for example, it is still a formal language with vocabulary and sentence structure.

There are a number of theories that speculate how humans first developed language, but my favorite is that of Shigeru Miyagawa, a professor of linguistics at the Massachusetts Institute of Technology. Miyagawa has built on the work of other linguists such as Noam Chomsky and Kenneth Hale; he argues that humans probably developed language as we know it by combining the gestural language of other animals with the songs of birds.

Gestural language is a wave of greeting or pointing to show a direction—think of the dance a bee performs to relay the location of pollen-rich flowers. We can understand the meaning of one gesture, like pointing, that's used in isolation, just as we understand the meaning of one word, like "fire."

But birdsong can't be picked apart. It is the expression layer. The message is communicated holistically. In other words, you need to hear the song in its entirety to understand its meaning; it dissolves into nonsense if you try to separate it into individual pieces, just as a hieroglyph loses its meaning if you pull out individual lines. Miyagawa believes that gestures and individual words were eventually not enough for us to communicate all that we wanted to say, so we added nuanced expression.

This is why Miyagawa's theory is my favorite—because it suggests that humans sang before they spoke.

We've forgotten how crucial communication is to our species, and that has perhaps made it easier to accept the disintegration of modern conversation. We may not realize how dependent we have been, historically, on our ability to communicate. It has been millennia since language and conversation became part of our survival. In that time, we have improved the tools for communication exponentially. But have we improved the communication itself? Have we improved what we say, how we say it, and how we receive what others tell us?

In a word: no.

There are two important reasons why we need to get better at talking to one another. One is economic; the other is human.

First, business: poor communication costs us about $37 billion a year, according to a study from training provider Cognisco.[4] That boils down to a tally, per worker, of more than $26,000 annually. And that calculation only includes companies with more than one hundred employees. Imagine how much higher that number would be if we included all businesses.

Good communication, on the other hand, is quite profitable. Companies with leaders who are great communicators have nearly 50 percent higher returns than companies with unexceptional communicators at the helm.[5] When retail giant Best Buy commissioned an in-depth study of the company's internal communications, one of the more notable insights gleaned was that for every percentage point the company increased employee engagement through communication, stores saw a $100,000 annual increase in operating income.

And according to research by Nobel Prize–winning

psychologist Daniel Kahneman, author of *Thinking, Fast and Slow*,[6] most people would rather do business with someone they like and trust than someone they dislike. I realize that may seem like a no-brainer, but get this: customers will choose a likable person over a less likable one, even if the likable person's product is lower quality *and* higher priced.

Here's another way to look at it: consumers in the United States return about $14 billion worth of electronics every year. But in 85 percent of those cases, there's nothing wrong with the merchandise. The consumer just doesn't understand how to use the device after opening the box. Sometimes weak documentation (such as an indecipherable instruction manual) is to blame; other times the culprit is insufficient "customer education," the formal term for the casual conversations salespeople have with customers about a product.

That translates to nearly $12 billion a year lost because instructions weren't clearly communicated. And in reality, this represents only a front-end loss because many consumers won't go back to a company after they've had to return a product they didn't understand how to use. Billions upon billions of dollars could be saved with good, clear communication.

The research on poor communication is extensive

and alarming. I mentioned earlier that lives are affected by communication in hospitals, but dollars are at stake there as well. Researchers at the University of Maryland found that so-called communication inefficiencies cost US hospitals about $12 billion every year.[7] That's a conservative estimate. It includes wasted time on the part of doctors and nurses, but over half of the cost stems from extra days that patients spend in the hospital because of information that wasn't shared in a timely or clear manner.

Communication also affects employee retention. No manager wants high turnover because it's expensive, regardless of the size of the business. It can cost more than $3,500 to replace one employee making $10 an hour.[8] A general rule of thumb is that it costs about 20 percent of an employee's annual salary to replace them. In other words, if the employee makes $35,000 per year, it will cost about $7,000 to replace that employee. So, losing an employee to miscommunication and lack of engagement is truly a waste of dollars and time.

But bad communication negatively affects our decisions on the front side of the hiring equation as well. I'm sure many HR administrators have had reason to think they hired the wrong candidate—but have they taken the time to figure out what went wrong? Hiring mistakes can sometimes be traced back to the job interview, to the questions that were asked and the responses that were offered. When it costs thousands to replace even a minimum-wage worker, those conversations can be measured in dollars and cents.

For example, a lot of hiring managers make the mistake of assuming that someone who talks well and a lot will be a good salesperson. The idea is that if someone is an entertaining storyteller, he or she must be great at seducing a client. But often the truth is just the opposite. Some of the most effective salespeople, the ones who sell the most, are those who can listen and respond.[9] Those who can hold good, balanced conversations are the ones who ultimately close the deal.

Our communication skills at work are not only shaky, they are also too seldom put to use. Many of us are guilty of firing off a quick e-mail when we could have walked down the hall to chat with a colleague or picked up the phone. Research shows that we are more likely to get our message across through conversation—either in person or on the phone—than we are using a written message. And yet, we avoid phone conversations so much that many large companies have decided to get rid of voice mail altogether. When JPMorgan Chase gave its employees the option to dump their voice mail in

2015, more than 65 percent of them did.[10] Coca-Cola made the same move in 2014 and only 6 percent of its employees opted to keep voice mail.

It's no surprise we have embraced texts and e-mails so readily. They're expedient, and they allow us to retain more control and maintain some distance—physical and emotional—from the person on the other end. We can respond when and if we like. We can edit before we send. We can save the e-mail and prove, months later, that we *did* send that memo to the IT department, no matter what anyone says to the contrary.

In our twenty-first-century business environment, it's natural to think these forms of communication are more efficient than a phone call. But research out of the McKinsey Global Institute suggests otherwise.[11] A 2012 study concluded that using e-mail more selectively and intentionally could increase productivity by 25 to 30 percent. (All of those blasted "Reply All" chains waste a lot of our time.) The phone doesn't necessarily help you work faster, says Ross McCammon of *Entrepreneur*. "This is about how the phone makes you work *better*. Because unlike email, the phone forces you to be more emphatic, more accurate, more honest."[12]

The effects of electronic communication trickle into our personal lives as well. A third of families say they argue over tech use on a daily basis, while half of American teens say they are addicted to their smartphones and tablets.[13] Sherry Turkle, MIT professor and author of *Reclaiming Conversation*, suggests young people wear headphones for the same reason adults overuse e-mail: we fear conversation. Turkle calls it the "Goldilocks effect." We want to connect with others, but we also want to remain in control: not too close, not too far, just right.

And that brings me to the other reason we need to talk—the human one. Paul Barnwell, a high school teacher who writes about education for the *Atlantic*, penned a piece in 2014 called "My Students Don't Know How to Have a Conversation."[14] "Conversational competence might be the single-most overlooked skill we fail to teach students," he wrote.

Kids spend hours each day engaging with ideas and one another through screens—but rarely do they have an opportunity to truly hone their interpersonal communication skills. Admittedly, teenage awkwardness and nerves play a role in difficult conversations. But students' reliance on screens for communication is detracting—and distracting—from their engagement in real-time talk. It might sound like a funny question, but we need to ask ourselves: Is there any 21st-century skill more important than being able to sustain confident, coherent conversation?

*　　*　　*

From the hallways of our high schools to employee break rooms to family dinner tables, our avoidance of conversation is taking a toll. By some measures, Americans are more polarized now than we have been since the Civil War.[15] I bet you're thinking, *what about the Vietnam War or the McCarthy era?* Nope, we agreed on more things during the Red Scare than we do today. A 2016 study by the Christian research group Q and the Maclellan Foundation found that most Americans now believe people who disagree with one another demonize one another so aggressively that it's impossible to find common ground.[16] And yet, that same study also revealed that most of us believe our society benefits from a wide diversity of opinions and perspectives. So while we value differing opinions in theory, we aren't very good at embracing them in real life.

Unfortunately, this trend is not limited to the United States. All across the globe, people are divided. We've seen evidence of this with the vote on Brexit in the UK, the ascension of an extreme-right presidential candidate in France, and the rise of extremist groups all throughout Europe.[17] Experts have measured high levels of polarization in all sixteen European countries, plus Japan, New Zealand, and Australia.[18] One reason for this division, I believe, is that no one really talks to each other anymore. And when we do converse face-to-face, we tend to talk *at* each other.

In a 2016 commencement address at Howard University, then president Barack Obama warned the graduating class against ideological isolation. "If you think that the only way forward is to be as uncompromising as possible," he said, "you will feel good about yourself, you will enjoy a certain moral purity, but you're not going to get what you want. So, don't try to shut folks out. Don't try to shut them down, no matter how much you might disagree with them."

And yet, we shut people out all the time. When we do connect, we usually seek out only those who already agree with our opinions.

We are not likely to solve problems at home or work or in government without discussion and compromise. That means that, in order for us not only to "get what we want" but also to advance as a species, we must reconnect with that which helps make us distinctly human. Technology will take us only so far; conversation can get us the rest of the way.

2

COMMUNICATION AND CONVERSATION ARE NOT THE SAME

The great enemy of communication, we find, is the illusion of it. We have talked enough; but we have not listened.

—WILLIAM WHYTE

A few years ago, my son was going through a tough time at school. He was being bullied, and he began to dread going to school each morning. He became reluctant to participate in class and stopped doing homework. His teacher e-mailed to let me know that his academic performance was suffering.

In the ensuing weeks, she and I exchanged a number of e-mails. I knew that this woman had my son's best interests at heart and I'm sure that, on some level, she knew the same about me. But we just weren't connecting. She was having trouble getting my son to do his work and probably thought I was making excuses for him. I felt like the one person I needed to help him couldn't see the full picture. And in the meantime, my son suffered.

Finally, I called the principal and asked to meet with him and the teacher. I'll admit it probably wasn't the best solution, because including her boss added pressure to the situation. The meeting started badly and quickly began to devolve into an argument. I knew that if we were going to help my son, I needed to appeal to this woman on an emotional level.

So, I consciously turned my body toward her so that her boss wasn't in my sight line. I reached out and touched her left hand on the table and I said, "I'm really sorry if I'm sometimes difficult to communicate with. I'm so concerned for my son. He only gets one chance at fourth grade. I apologize if anything I've said has come off as angry. I just want him to have a good year in school and I can't bear to see him in so much pain."

I saw her face soften. I watched the hard lines beside her mouth relax and disappear, something I could never have seen in an e-mail. And she said, "Don't worry, Celeste. I'm pulling for him. I'm on his side all the way and I'll do everything I can to make sure he's successful. And you know what? He's a great kid. I really love him."

From that moment forward, this teacher became my son's strongest advocate. Like any other parent, I have had many, many conversations with my kid's teachers over the years, but that one stands out because the effects were so dramatic. We had been communicating for weeks from behind screens, but we hadn't connected as human beings.

I can't speak for what was inside her mind during that time, but I can say that I had started to think of her as a job title and not a person. She was my son's teacher, not a young woman who worked sixteen-hour days to handle a crowded class of kids. For too long, I saw her not as an idealist paying off student loans for an education degree that had earned her a relatively low-wage job working with children but as an obstacle to my kid's success.

All it took was one conversation for us to fully see each other.

Our use of technology has exploded in the past decade. In 2000, we sent about 14 billion texts every month. By 2010, that number rose to 188 billion. And by 2014, it was 561 billion texts. In fourteen years, the number of texts we sent increased by 547 billion. That's an incredible leap. And it's echoed in the statistics on e-mail. In 2011, there were about 105 billion e-mails sent. By 2020, that number is expected to be 246 billion.[1]

Lest you think this is a first-world problem, the data shows that this growth is occurring all over the world, in both developed and developing nations. In a 2012 survey of twenty-one countries, Pew Research found that 75 percent of people who own cell phones use them to text.[2] Two of the places where texting is most common are among the poorest nations: Kenya and Indonesia. Our reliance on technology is changing the way everyone communicates.

What effect does this have on our conversational skills? The truth is, we don't yet have a complete understanding of that. Research into the effects of texting, for example, is evolving daily. And, of course, correlation is not causation; we can detect changes in social behavior that have occurred since the smartphone revolution, but it's difficult to prove that one thing caused the other.

That said, there's a strong indication that the rise of technology, social media, and texting has led to a decrease in a few critical components of effective communication.

One of those components is empathy. In 2010, a team at the University of Michigan compiled the results of seventy-two studies conducted over thirty years.[3] They found a 40 percent decline in empathy among college students, with the vast majority of that decline taking place after 2000. "The ease of having 'friends' online might make people more likely to just tune out when they don't feel like responding to others' problems," noted an author of the study, "a behavior that could carry over offline."

I find this development to be extremely worrisome. Empathy, at its most basic, is the ability to sense someone else's feelings, to be aware of their emotional state, and to imagine their experience. Not just to recognize that a coworker is sad, but to imagine what he or she may be going through and what it would feel like if you were going through the same thing.

To experience empathy, we must establish a connection between our idea of ourselves and of another person. We have to ask questions like, "Would I like it if that happened to me?" "How would I feel if someone ran over my mailbox?" Or, in my case, "How must it feel to be responsible for twenty-five fourth-grade students every day?"

Empathy is a critical human ability. Even babies as young as six months old show signs of empathic behavior. In their book *White Racism*, sociologists Pinar Batur, Joe Feagin, and Hernán Vera wrote, "Empathy is an essential component of human social life. Empathy tells us that a child's cry means discomfort or hunger. Empathy allows us to relate pleasure to a smile and pain to lament. Empathy permits us to come together and communicate."[4]

There's no arguing that empathy is an essential element of meaningful communication. But the ways in which we communicate today offer few opportunities for empathic connection. One recent study of our social media use suggested that nearly half of online friendships are "non-reciprocal."[5] That is, half of the people you identify as your "friends" online do not feel the same way about you. One participant in the study supplied a list of people they could call in an emergency, and when the researcher contacted them, only half said they'd actually be inclined to help.

Some experts say human nature is inherently optimistic and that's why we think some relationships are deeper than they are. Others suggest we've become more opportunistic about these relationships since accruing large numbers of "friends" has become a social (and sometimes professional) aspiration. The word "friend" is now a verb and we describe certain people as "Twitter friends," meaning we only know them 140 characters at a time.

Ronald Sharp, a professor of English at Vassar College, coauthored *The Norton Book of Friendship* with his lifelong confidante, Eudora Welty. He touched on this evolving definition of friendship in a 2016 interview with the *New York Times*. "Treating friends like investments or commodities is anathema to the whole idea of friendship," Sharp said. "It's not about what someone can do for you, it's who and what the two of you become in each other's presence. The notion of doing nothing but spending time in each other's company has, in a way, become a lost art. People are so eager to maximize efficiency of relationships [through texts and tweets] that they have lost touch with what it is to be a friend."[6]

As Sharp points out, meaningful connection requires an investment of time. Conversations are uniquely human and, like us, they are complicated and sometimes chaotic and often rambling. That's why another essential ingredient for good conversation is attention.

Computers can relay information in milliseconds, but human beings cannot and should not attempt to mimic this efficiency. Most of the time, it's the tangents and offhand remarks that reveal the most about someone. It may take five minutes for your friend to relay a simple story about a trip to the grocery store, but it's the pauses and the smiles and the bursts of laughter that make the story memorable. If you can't pay attention long enough to listen to the whole thing, you'll miss all of that.

And a lot of us do miss those details since today, the average human attention span is about eight seconds—on par with that of a goldfish.[7] Even at work, our ability to focus on any one task for long is diminished. The average worker is interrupted every three minutes by e-mails, phone calls, texts, and social media.

It's likely that the Internet is a major cause of our shrinking attention span, and it's shrunk more quickly since we started taking the Internet everywhere we go via smartphones and tablets. In fact, research has shown that even the mere presence of these gadgets negatively impacts face-to-face conversation.

In one study, British researchers asked pairs of strangers to sit down in a room and chat. In half of the rooms, a cell phone was placed on a nearby table; in the other half, no phone was present. After the conversations had ended, the researchers asked study participants what they thought of each other. Here's what they learned: when a cell phone was present in the room, the participants reported that the quality of their relationship was worse than those who'd talked in a cell phone–free room. The pairs who talked in the rooms with cell phones "also reported feeling less trust and thought their partners showed less empathy if there was a cell phone present."[8]

The researchers concluded that the presence of a cell phone hurt the quality of the conversation and the strength of the connection between the people talking. With a cell phone just sitting on a table in the room!

Think of all the times you've sat down to have lunch with a friend or colleague and set your phone on the table. You might have felt virtuous because you didn't pick it up to check your e-mail, but your ignored messages were still undermining your connection with the person sitting across from you.

Even if we can manage to keep our phones in our pockets, pay attention to the person talking to us for more than eight seconds, and muster up some empathy to forge an emotional connection, there's one more obstacle that technology presents: our willingness to have a conversation in the first place.

A 2014 Pew Research study found that people are less likely to share their views in person if they've discovered that their opinions aren't popular on social media.[9] It's an ironic development, given that in its early days, it was widely speculated that social media would serve as an inclusive forum for more diverse perspectives. But in practice, fear of disagreement online is shutting down the potential for lively conversations.

Don't get me wrong; I'm not anti-tech. I own a tablet and a smartphone and a laptop and an e-reader. I have a Samsung watch that lets me speak into it (like Dick Tracy) or e-mail my son from my wrist. If he doesn't check his e-mail fast enough, I can send that same message to his phone or tablet with a few swipes of my finger.

Technology-enabled communication can be a wonderful thing, and it's true that initiating conversation is messier and riskier than firing off an e-mail or a text. But the mess is often the best part. Think of a young man's stumbling declaration of love or a little girl's breathless description of her first day at school. These nuances are lost on a screen. While typing up our thoughts and editing them carefully grant us some measure of control, I don't think we get the best end of the deal. We may gain convenience, but we often lose the most powerful part of the message we transmit: the emotion behind it.

While I was writing this book, I used a planner (so analog!) to keep a running tally of my face-to-face conversations each day. Before this exercise, I estimated that I probably had three or four substantive conversations a day. But after tracking them carefully, it turned out that most days I was having perhaps one or two, sometimes none. It felt like more because I was communicating with people all day. But I was rarely talking with them.

I'm not a scientist, but I can use scientific methods to observe how my relationships, and the conversations I have, are impacted by technology. We can all do this field research by tracking how often we converse face-to-face as opposed to text or e-mail. And we can be more aware, while we're chatting in line at the grocery store or across from each other at the lunch table, of our ability to empathize and develop a true connection.

It's a truism that you learn more about yourself in practice than in theory, and that means once you've finished reading this book, you must go out and converse. You can't learn to ride a bike by reading about it. Biking is active and requires practice. The same is true of conversation. Thinking about it is not enough.

3

YOU CAN'T OUTSMART A
BAD CONVERSATION

We are taught you must blame your father, your sisters, your brothers, the school, the teachers—but never blame yourself. It's never your fault. But it's always your fault, because if you wanted to change you're the one who has got to change.

—KATHARINE HEPBURN

I'm often approached by people who've heard me speak or watched my TED talk. Nine out of ten times, if they have a question, it's about how to deal with other people and their awful conversation skills. "What if someone else won't stop talking?" "What if that person is really boring and keeps repeating themselves?" "What if they hardly say anything?"

Here are a couple of questions I almost never hear: "I always interrupt people. How do I stop doing that?" "I get bored when other people talk. Can I change that?" We tend to blame bad conversations on other people. Awkwardness on a first date? The other person isn't a very good talker. Heated fight at the dinner table? Your uncle is an ignorant bully.

Most people think that they're pretty good at this stuff already. If you're reading this book, you probably recognize that there's room for improvement, but chances are you think you're better than average at conversation. I get it. I thought that, too. It took a few spectacular failures to make me accept that I could use some help in this area.

One of my more memorable failures took place at work. I'd scheduled a meeting with my boss to talk about a situation that I found untenable. I needed to somehow explain that a coworker's behavior had crossed the line from annoying to abusive, and I knew it wasn't going to be easy. It's one thing when someone steals from you, hits you, or calls you an offensive name. But talking about behavioral nuance—often called microaggression—is more challenging.

So I prepared carefully. I read articles on how to have difficult conversations at work. I even rehearsed with my spouse.

"He's going to say that there's no malice intended," my husband told me. "So, what do you say to that?"

"I'll say it's not an isolated incident but a longstanding pattern of behavior," I answered.

"He'll say he was kidding."

"I will say that the effect of continued inappropriate jokes is far from humorous and can't be explained away by telling me to 'lighten up.'"

Needless to say, I felt ready as I walked into my boss's office. I was nervous, but I was also confident. I had done my homework. I had notes. I had specific examples. I *had* it.

Except I didn't.

When I sat down, I noticed that my palms were sweaty—and they're almost never sweaty, even at the gym. I stated my case as I'd rehearsed, but my boss's response wasn't at all what I expected. I was derailed immediately. As I struggled to articulate a response, he started asking about my state of mind. Was I tired? Stressed? Overwhelmed?

I was caught off guard. Yes, I was feeling stressed. No, I wasn't sleeping well. I kept returning to my mental notes, to the version of this conversation that I had so carefully planned, but it didn't help in the least. My boss had effectively turned the entire conversation into a discussion of my mood and work habits. I was on the defensive. I walked out with an appointment to meet with a coach who could help me cope at work. My manager had no intention of speaking to the colleague with whom I had an issue.

I had solved nothing, I hadn't been heard, and I didn't

listen because I was completely focused on moving back to the conversation I had envisioned. Not only did I not accomplish what I intended, but that conversation ultimately escalated a problem that I wanted to de-escalate. I became more frustrated, more stressed, and had no recourse because I wasn't going to go back to my boss a second time.

I left that job mere months later. There were certainly other factors involved in my departure, but that conversation, and the problems it worsened rather than addressed, was a significant driver.

Here's the thing, and the main reason I think that disastrous discussion had such a profound impact on me: I really should have owned that conversation. For once, I was fully prepared and I expected to achieve a specific goal. Plus, I'm a professional talker. By all objective measures, I'm better at conversation than the majority of people. At that point, I'd been a radio reporter and anchor for about twelve years. I'd studied with some of the best interview coaches in the business, participated in prestigious fellowships, read dozens of guides. I had even done interviews with experts on the subject of conversation. I'd talked with people who had studied human conversation for years. I should have been better at communication than most people. But I wasn't.

That day was an eye-opener for me. Over the course of my journalism career, I'd read about people who are bad conversationalists. I hadn't known that I was one of them. I'd sat through workshops, listening to stories about hapless reporters who got rolled over in interviews and lost control while the guest dominated the exchange. I had laughed smugly. But guess what? People who get rolled over often don't see the roller coming. They may not see it at all until it's on top of them, smooshing them into the dirt.

Good conversation doesn't happen naturally, though most of us assume the opposite. It's true, most of us have been stringing together words since age two or three. The problem is, most of us have spent all those decades in between getting a lot of practice at the wrong things. We've been repeating the same mistakes our whole lives.

Unfortunately, few of us are aware of this problem. In fact, we tend to rate our conversational competence as much higher than it really is, no matter whether we're at work, school, or sitting at home. And the data backs this up—numerous studies have found that our perception of our own communication skills is not very accurate. Cornell University's David Dunning, a social psychologist, says that for most people it is "intrinsically difficult to get a sense of what [they] don't know." After more than a decade of research, Dunning concluded that "people tend to hold overly favorable views of their abilities in many social and intellectual domains."[1]

Research also suggests that smart people are very often bad communicators. And the smarter you are, the worse you may be. I like to think I'm fairly smart. (I think it's okay to say that. Believe me, I spend my days talking to people who remind me that I'm not the smartest person in the room. When you regularly interview astrophysicists and neuroscientists and Pulitzer Prize–winning novelists, your rung on the smart ladder is apparent.) I'm also what's called a "creative." I'm a professional opera singer, with multiple degrees in music. I've always thought that being smart and being creative meant I was better at communicating than most people. More specifically, I thought that because I was *articulate*, I was also good in conversations. But that's absolutely not true. Being a good talker doesn't make you a good listener, and being smart might make you a terrible listener.

Highly educated people also tend to place a great deal of value on logic and discount the importance of emotion. You can't win a debate with an emotional argument, of course, but conversation is not debate and human beings are inherently illogical. We are emotional creatures. To remove, or attempt to remove, emotion from your conversation is to extract a great deal of meaning and import.

For example, sometimes we use facts to respond to emotion. A friend starts to talk about his pending divorce, and we console him with, "Don't feel bad. Almost half of marriages end in divorce anyway," or we say, "Don't worry. One psychologist says divorce can actually improve your kids' chances at a lasting healthy relationship."[2] Both of those things are true, but they're completely unhelpful to your friend who needs emotional support. A conversation is not a college lecture course or a TED talk. No matter how awkward it may feel to be on the listening end of someone's heartbreak, escaping into logic is rarely the right response.

Think about some of the stereotypical refrains offered up to people who share their pain. "There are plenty of other fish in the sea" may be true, both literally and figuratively, but I doubt it has ever comforted someone who's just been dumped. "That job wasn't a good fit for you anyway" or "You're disturbing everyone in the restaurant" or "Crying won't help" have probably never consoled anyone, either. Approaching emotional problems with logic is a strategy that is doomed to failure.

Logic attempts to negate emotion, but emotion is not weakness, nor is it unhelpful. Humans are social animals and our emotions are both useful and important. A good conversation requires its participants to use their IQ and their EQ.

Logic isn't as ironclad as you might suspect, anyway. We make logical errors constantly, and especially when we're conversing. That's because when we talk to other people, we often rely on what Daniel Kahneman calls System 1 thinking. System 1 thinking is quick, intuitive, and relies heavily on patterns we've learned after years of experience.

For example, let's say you see a dirty and disheveled man sitting on the ground outside of a subway station. System 1 thinking tells you he is homeless. Or imagine that you text your partner saying you'll be several hours late getting home from work and you receive one or two words in response: System 1 thinking tells you that your partner is angry.

System 1 thinking is not always wrong and it serves an important purpose of simplifying our decisions so that we don't spend unnecessary time overthinking every choice. It brings calm to chaos by reducing the amount of data our mind has to sift through. However, System 1 is also easily duped because it relies on assumptions.

System 1 is also quite emotional—it bases decisions on stereotypes—so even when we think we're being logical, we often are not.

Kahneman illustrated this point by presenting students at Harvard, MIT, and Princeton with the following math problem:

A baseball bat and ball, together, cost $1.10.

The bat costs $1.00 more than the ball.

How much does the ball cost?

More than half of the bright students at those elite institutions answered this problem incorrectly. The correct answer is 5 cents, because the bat costs a dollar *more* than the ball. So, 5 cents plus a dollar is $1.05 and, together, the bat and ball would be $1.10.

Here's another problem that Kahneman and his cohorts presented to these students: There is a patch of lily pads on a lake. Each day, the patch doubles in size. It takes forty-eight days for the lily pads to cover the lake completely, so how long does it take for the lily pads to cover half of the lake?

The correct answer is forty-seven because the patch doubles in size every day. So, if it covers the entire lake on the forty-eighth day, then it must be covering half of the lake the day before. Most people, though, simply divide 48 by 2 because they read the word "doubles."

Our experience with patterns tells us that the opposite of doubling is dividing in half.

The reason most people get those problems wrong, according to Kahneman, is that they rely on System 1 thinking. Remember that Kahneman is a psychologist, not a mathematician. He was researching why smart people get so much wrong, not why they do badly on math quizzes. Most people use mental shortcuts to find answers to problems. Even when we think we're being analytical, our assumptions and shortcuts quite often lead us to the wrong answer not just in math problems, but also in our human relationships.

Kahneman's research indicates that smart people are wrong to assume they're free from bias or less prone to it than others. And the belief that your intelligence protects you from erroneous assumptions may actually make you more vulnerable to them. That's certainly true in conversation, where our logic is sometimes inadequate and our assumptions are frequently incorrect.

Intelligence also gets in the way of good conversation because smart people can be reluctant to ask for help. They're supposed to be brighter and more articulate than the average person, and if they are talking to an employee, a child, a student, or anyone who they consider to be less intelligent or less educated, it's unlikely they'll admit they don't understand something. Conversation is supposed to come naturally, after all. Even toddlers can carry on a two-way dialogue. Acknowledging that you don't understand something another person is trying to tell you can feel like an admission of weakness or an acceptance of the fact that you're not quite as smart as you'd like to believe.

I encourage you to consider what you bring to the table in your conversations. Our perception of how well we communicate is often quite different from reality. The next time you are part of a conversation that goes awry, ask for feedback. Let the other person know that the exchange didn't go as you hoped and you wonder if you could have phrased things differently, or if you were focused on the wrong things, or if you didn't understand their point. Then listen. Listen to what they have to say without taking offense. Maybe start with someone you know well, like a sibling or a friend. Listening to constructive criticism is never easy, but if your goal is to become better at conversations, it's important to get an honest assessment of the areas most in need of improvement.

I know that once I admitted that I was at least half of the problem, I finally began to recognize where I was going wrong. I talked to people in my radio studio and then listened back to what mistakes I made and which opportunities I missed. Not surprisingly, I found that as my skills improved, my conversations both inside and outside of my studio improved as well. As I became better at listening, the shy talkers spoke up more. As I became more focused, the chatterboxes stopped rambling on.

In conversations, as in life, you can't control what someone else does or says; you can only control yourself. But sometimes, that's enough.

One of my favorite radio guests is the novelist Salman Rushdie. I've interviewed him more often than any other person in my almost twenty-year career. What I like about him is that he really listens to my questions and takes care to answer what I've asked. Sometimes, he even thinks for a moment before he answers. You'd be surprised at how rare that is, especially in a business where many people come armed with "talking points."

In my most recent interview with him, I mentioned that critics rarely talk about how funny his books are. "There are a lot of jokes," I said, "I mean, out-and-out jokes, and I wonder if you're ever sitting there thinking, 'Oh, I better take this joke out because I am literature with a capital L.'" And he answers, "I really have no sense of being literature with a capital L . . . I like books that are funny, to speak as a reader. I have some difficulty with even the greatest books if they are completely lacking in a sense of humor, and I'm looking at you, George Eliot." And then we both laugh and I say, "I enjoyed it but it is a slog." And Rushdie says, "Yeah, [there are] no gags in *Middlemarch*." (How do you not enjoy a Booker Prize–winning novelist who talks about missing "gags" in George Eliot? I can't get enough of that guy.)

When I began to work on my conversation skills, I asked myself: Am I doing the things Mr. Rushdie does that make him such a delight to speak with? Was I listening to what people said and then responding, or did I simply wait for them to take a breath so I could say the clever thing I'd already formulated in my mind? After my third interview with the novelist, I started to take note of how often I listened closely before I responded. I realized I hadn't really been listening to him, and that meant that we didn't really have a conversation. I had just been asking unconnected questions, crafted in advance, unchanged by his answers.

It's easy to turn a blind eye to our communication weaknesses; we tend to make exceptions and excuses for our mistakes, and sometimes even go so far as to recast our weaknesses into strengths. For example, you may not enjoy making small talk with your neighbors at the end of a long day, but you tell yourself that the reason you avoid eye contact with the guy next door is because you respect everyone's privacy. Or let's say you're reluctant to engage with your colleagues at the office. You may tell yourself it's because you don't want to interrupt them when they're working or because you're too focused on your own work to waste time, but the truth is you may not care what the person in the adjacent cubicle did over the weekend.

We have an amazing capacity to justify almost any action that we want to take or avoid. Pat Wagner, a management and communication consultant at Pattern Research, refers to these justifications as "virtuous flaws." Of course, we rarely extend the same courtesy to others. We don't talk to people on the elevator but say of a coworker, "She's so cold! When I pass her in the hall, she barely says hello." Wagner says we are frequently oblivious to how poor our interpersonal skills are and how they affect other people. We don't know or don't care that our tendency to interrupt is discouraging others from speaking up in meetings or that our failure to remember details makes people anxious.

Here's an exercise I used to try to get over this perception problem. (It's based on something that Wagner does in her workshops.) I made a list of the things people do in conversation that bother me. Do they repeat themselves? Ramble on? Interrupt? I wrote it all down. Then, I took that list to my friends and coworkers and asked them how many of those things they think I do. I asked if I do those things often or just once in a while.

I made sure to impress upon them that I was looking for absolute honesty because the purpose of the exercise was to improve my skills and I promised not to be offended by their answers. This was a scary enterprise, but a very, very enlightening one.

Of course, you can never know all that you need to know about talking with other people, and every conversation will present its own challenges and rewards. As author Joshua Uebergang says, "Communication skills are not information." You can't memorize them like the elements in the periodic table and gain mastery. And yet, that's how most of us approach it.

When you go looking for advice on how to enjoy better conversations, you'll often find tips that are meant to be applied broadly to any situation. You are probably familiar with some of these strategies already—tired tidbits like maintain eye contact, come armed with interesting topics to discuss, repeat back what you've heard, smile and nod to show that you're paying attention, and sometimes say "uh-huh" and "yeah" as an encouragement.

Here is my advice: don't do any of those things! I don't care what expert told you it was a good idea, it's most often not. Why should you heed *my* advice? Because the studio where I broadcast each day functions as a kind of conversational laboratory. Just as a chemist experiments with silver nitrate or acetone or chlorine, I sit down with dozens of people every week and experiment with different kinds of conversations. Most of these people are strangers to me, from all over the world, from all different walks of life. I've talked to senators and movie stars, carpenters and truck drivers, billionaires and kindergarten teachers. Some of them are highly emotional; some are quite detached. My studio is a perfect place to test out techniques.

When I encounter a piece of advice like, "Nod your head and say 'uh-huh' to show you're paying attention," I can take that tip into my studio (lab) and try it out. I can nod and say "uh-huh" to dozens of people and take note of their reactions. Does it work? In fact, it does not.

What I found is that consciously nodding your head is inauthentic and reads that way to the person you're facing. If I nod my head naturally and unconsciously, without trying to do so, the other person responds positively. But if I'm strategizing and thinking to myself, "I should nod to demonstrate that I'm paying attention,"

I don't often get a warm response. That's probably because I had to stop paying attention to the conversation in order to think consciously about nodding and pretending to be engaged. I watched a video of myself recently doing a news interview in which I was using this little pearl of wisdom. I looked like an idiot. Only a professional actor can make a fake nod look genuine. The rest of us look like bobbleheads.

The "maintain eye contact" strategy is also unhelpful, or worse. When I tried it out in a job interview, the human resources representative asked unironically if I had drunk too much coffee. "You seem really intense," she said, with a nervous laugh. Not the intended effect.

After trying out just about every piece of conversation advice out there—and finding that most of it feels contrived or unrealistic in practice—I began to question my assumptions about what makes for good communication. Maybe, I thought, much of what I'd learned over a lifetime was wrong. Maybe the strategies I'd memorized and mastered weren't as helpful as I'd thought. I had to strip away all my years of training and start with a blank slate. I had to admit that when it came to conversation, maybe I wasn't as smart as I thought I was.

4

SET THE STAGE

If you align expectations with reality, you will never be disappointed.

—TERRELL OWENS

I used to host a show called *Front Row Center* at WDET in Detroit. It was a weekly show that focused on arts and culture in the Motor City. When I say "culture," I'm not just talking about museums and theater. I also reported on books about hiking to the Antarctic and the history of traffic lights, the perils of suburban sprawl and new ideas in automotive design.

At one point, I had gathered a panel to talk about environmental activism and race. While people of color make up about 40 percent of the American population, they represent only 12 to 15 percent of the staff at environmental groups.[1] I wondered why, and I invited the CEO of a building company to talk with me about it (a white male), the chief of an environmental group (a white female), and an African American woman who led a community group and could talk about what was needed in order to recruit more people of color.

We had a total of twenty minutes or so to talk. I started off with a question to the contractor about diversity and asked how many African Americans worked at his company. Then, I threw a follow-up question to the environmentalist, asking if she saw similar numbers at her group. While she was answering, the third guest ripped the headphones from her head, threw them on a table, and stalked out of the room in a huff. I'm talking about the kind of huff that's basically silent but is designed to leave no doubt in anyone's mind about the person's frustration.

The interview wasn't live, so I had two options: I could excuse myself from the studio, follow the woman out, and ask what was bothering her. Or I could let her go and continue the conversation without her. I chose the latter option.

The woman who walked out penned a letter to my boss, suggesting that I didn't allow her to speak because I was racist. He responded that the interview was only ninety seconds into the conversation when she walked away and also that I am multiracial and, therefore, probably not prejudiced against blacks. But there was no moral high ground for either of us to occupy. I was facilitating a discussion about access for minorities and the only person of color in the room (besides myself) felt unwelcome and disrespected.

That moment still bothers me. I can't help but think I missed an opportunity. Maybe I should have asked her a question first, but I was trying to establish the severity of the problem before talking about the causes. Maybe I should have run after her. I never saw her again after she walked out of the studio, and I regret that.

I've done thousands of interviews in my career, had thousands of conversations, and most of them didn't end with someone walking out and calling me a racist (although Congressman Barney Frank has hung up on me a couple of times). And yet, it's the failures that stay with me. Isn't that how it is for most of us? Don't we gnaw away at failed conversations like a dog with a bone, going over what was said and what we could have done differently?

I never could make sense of that failure until years later when another guest, a professor, became irate because his interview was so short. He had come to the studio prepared to talk for fifteen minutes, but we were done after five, and he was furious. One of my producers laughed about it. He thought it was a silly thing to get upset about. "Doesn't he understand the news business?" my producer asked.

I tried to put myself in the professor's shoes. I thought

about how he must have spent a couple of days preparing for his interview, writing notes and checking his facts. He might have practiced with his wife or partner. He may have gotten up early that morning to dress carefully and go over his research. He'd imagined how the interview would go, what he would say. Then, it ended so quickly that he didn't have time to say all of the important stuff that he'd prepared so carefully.

He was angry because he had specific expectations and those expectations weren't met. And that may have been what angered the woman on the environmental panel as well. She was looking forward to the conversation, she had high expectations, and she was immediately disappointed when it didn't go as she'd envisioned.

People get upset when their expectations aren't met—no surprise there. At first, I couldn't see how I could do anything to mitigate that. After all, I can't prevent someone from having expectations. I can't know what those expectations are, and, even if I did, I couldn't possibly accommodate them all on a live radio show.

Then one morning, a young woman walked into my studio for her first live interview. She sat down in front of the mic, rubbing her hands up and down her thighs and taking repeated sips from her water bottle.

"Are you a little nervous?" I asked.

"More than a little," she said.

"There's nothing to be afraid of. Just look at me, try to forget there's a microphone in front of you, and we'll have a friendly conversation."

"Do you think you could walk me through exactly how it all works? Just tell me, step by step, how the interview is going to go? I'll feel better if I know what to expect."

There it was. Knowing what to expect made her feel more comfortable and more secure. I didn't need to change her expectations; she did that herself once I gave her the information she needed. I told her my expectations and she adjusted her own. We went on to have a fantastic interview.

Think about your favorite doctor for a moment. What does he or she do that puts you at ease? The doctor probably has a calm demeanor and explains everything that's about to happen ("We'll give you an X-ray to see if the bone is fractured"), whether it's going to hurt ("You might feel a slight pinch"), and what the next steps are ("If there's no fracture, you have probably pulled a muscle and we'll need to wrap it").

This is one of the most important lessons I've learned as a journalist: explain what you want and what you expect, and be honest. When my guests sit down, I say,

"I'm going to read a short intro and then introduce you. We have about twelve minutes to talk and that will go by quickly, so try to keep your answers focused and brief. If you see me start to nod at you or hold up my finger, it's time to end the segment, so just wrap up what you're saying." Those few sentences make all the difference between a nervous guest who doesn't know what's going to happen and a more relaxed guest who feels that everything is under control.

Even off the air, I've found this strategy lays the groundwork for better conversations. For example, when I had to discipline an employee at work recently, I stated the purpose of our meeting immediately. I said, "I've called you in to give you an official reprimand. But that's as severe as this gets. You're in no danger of being fired. I want to start this discussion by saying how valuable you are to me and the company. My goal is to help you succeed and make you aware of some issues that might be holding you back." Months later, he made the changes he needed to make and even earned a pay raise.

When I have to scold my son, I try not to lead up to it or ask passive-aggressive questions like, "What did I tell you to do this morning?" I simply say, "I'm angry with you because you forgot to take the trash out again. Before you leave, you need to do it." And because he's the most perfect kid in the world, he gets up, takes out the trash, and vows that he'll never neglect to do so again. Yeah, that's what happens.

Of course, you first have to *know* what you want before you can express those expectations to someone else. And that's what makes this strategy so useful. It forces you to think about the objectives of the conversation in advance and articulate what you want to the other person. When you're confiding in a friend, are you simply looking for a shoulder to cry on or do you want advice? Tell the other person, so he or she doesn't feel the need to solve your problem. When you're irritated with your partner because of a specific grievance, do you just need to express your frustration, or do you need to have a conversation about how to avoid a repeat offense?

Taking a moment to think about your own expectations and sharing them with your conversational partner sets the stage for a productive exchange. It's the equivalent of walking into the grocery store with a list instead of browsing through the aisles; you're much more likely to get what you need and leave feeling satisfied.

Articulating expectations is one of the simplest ways to set the stage for an effective conversation, but there are a few other methods for creating a productive and fertile environment. One is to take a moment to consider how you're feeling before you initiate an important discussion.

Earlier, I denigrated the use of body language techniques, like intentionally nodding your head or constantly maintaining eye contact. While I do think that most of the communication advice centered on body language is unhelpful and counterproductive, authentic, natural gestures and tone often reveal our true feelings. If I'm thinking about something that disgusts me while I'm talking about love, for example, people will pick up—sometimes subconsciously—on the disgust and not the affection.

Likewise, if you're feeling anxious, distracted, angry, or simply stressed out, all of those feelings will change the tone of your voice and expression on your face. I have to admit that this is a real problem for me: every thought that passes through my mind is instantly broadcast on my face. That's the reason I'm a terrible liar and a spectacularly bad poker player. You'd think it wouldn't matter in radio, since the audience can't see my face, but the expert or politician I'm interviewing can see me and knows exactly what I'm thinking.

We bring expectations to every conversation, no matter how brief. That's what is going on in our heads before either person opens their mouth to speak. We can't always control how a conversation goes, but we can create an environment for open, authentic communication by sharing our expectations and being aware of our own thoughts and feelings before we decide to speak. We can fertilize the ground before we plant the seeds.

The rest of this book will focus on how we can converse better, but I would suggest that what happens before the conversation is just as important. Set the stage for a successful, enjoyable exchange by checking to make sure you're both there to see the same show.

5

SOME CONVERSATIONS ARE HARDER THAN OTHERS

I suppose I flee to life. I'm most interested when conversations become difficult.

—TAMSIN GREIG

I've been told many times in recent years that there are some people "you just can't talk to." One person told me she can't speak to anyone who won't acknowledge the existence of institutional racism. Another said that if someone he knew supported a particular presidential candidate, then "we have nothing in common and nothing to say to each other." These days, it seems that there are more and more deal breakers than ever when it comes to who we're willing to talk to. And yet, the need to have difficult conversations has never been greater.

A good conversation is not necessarily an easy one. There are subjects so sensitive and topics so emotionally charged that discussions about them can be tricky and even dangerous. But there is not a human being on this planet with whom you have "nothing in common." And there is no topic so volatile that it can't be spoken of.

Let me tell you the story of an African American girl, born eighty-five years ago in Muskogee, Oklahoma. She was a twin, the daughter of a minister, and her name was Xernona (pronounced "zer-NO-nuh"). She moved to Atlanta in 1965 to work for the Southern Christian Leadership Conference, or SCLC, the civil rights group whose first president was Dr. Martin Luther King Jr. Xernona worked closely with Dr. King and became close friends with his wife, Coretta.

Xernona worked hard to desegregate Atlanta's hospitals so that sick and wounded patients wouldn't have to be transported miles away to an institution that catered to their race. Her work was noticed by the mayor of the city, Ivan Allen Jr., and he appointed her to lead the Model Cities program. That program was a part of President Lyndon Johnson's Great Society. Its goal was to improve poor neighborhoods and foster a new generation of black civic leaders.

As head of Model Cities in Atlanta, Xernona oversaw five different communities and each of those communities had a chairperson. When she started her work, Mayor Allen warned her about one of those chairs, Calvin Craig. Craig, at that time, was a grand dragon in the Georgia

Realm of the United Klans of America, Knights of the Ku Klux Klan. Xernona recalled years later that, during her first meeting with the chairpeople, one man gave her just the tips of his fingers in a handshake and she thought, "He must be the one."[1]

Over the course of the next year or so, Xernona and Calvin ended up talking almost every day, not just about race but about all kinds of things. For some reason, Calvin Craig kept returning to her downtown Atlanta office.

And so they would sit and chat, always friendly and always respectful. She says he never called her by her first name. "I mean, he acted so gentlemanly, and we would have such laughter," Xernona says. "And I asked, 'Why do you keep coming here? You and I don't agree on anything.' He said, 'Ha, ha. Oh, Mrs. Clayton, you're fun to talk to.'"

If you were unaware that Clayton and Craig were talking so often, it must have been a stunning development when Calvin Craig held a press conference in April 1968 to announce that he was leaving the KKK. He said he would henceforward dedicate his life to building a nation in which "black men and white men can stand shoulder to shoulder in a united America."[2]

Like most stories, this one is more complicated than

it appears on the surface. Craig would eventually rejoin the KKK, only to quit again years later. But it is not an exaggeration to say that Xernona talked him out of his racism. Craig himself credited her with his conversion and his daughter, forty-three years after her father's historic press conference, called Xernona and begged to see her. "I came here especially to thank you," she said when they met, "because you healed my father and cleansed our family." Xernona has explained that she didn't set out to change Craig's mind. Dr. King had told her, "You've got to change a man's heart before you can change his behavior."

I love this story because it exemplifies the power of conversation between two people who are willing to listen to and learn from each other. It shows us how transformative conversation can be. It's also a response to all of the people who claim they "just can't" talk to someone else because their opinions are too offensive.

If an African American woman can talk respectfully and openly with a grand dragon in the KKK, I find it hard to believe that you can't talk to the guy in the coffee shop who's wearing a Trump T-shirt or the woman in your office who can't stop talking about her vegan diet.

At the same time, it's obviously true that some conversations are harder than others. Some topics are riskier and carry a higher danger of offending someone or hurting their feelings. So, let me offer some tried-and-true methods for having a difficult exchange without getting into an argument.

Through my experience and research, I've identified five key strategies that help facilitate a productive dialogue. They are: be curious, check your bias, show respect, stay the course, and end well.

The first component, being curious, speaks to a genuine willingness to learn something from someone else. Xernona Clayton didn't talk to Craig with the intention of educating him or convincing him that he was wrong. She was curious to know what was behind his beliefs, to get to know the person who held opinions that threatened her very existence.

In 2016, former Central Intelligence Agency clandestine service officer Amaryllis Fox gave a somewhat controversial interview to Al Jazeera. Some took issue with her characterization of the war on terror, but I think her remarks are extremely valuable for the student of conversation.

Fox explained how she was able to talk with terrorists and extremists in her work. "Everybody believes they are the good guy," she said. "The only real way to disarm your enemy is to listen to them. If you hear them out, if you're brave enough to really listen to their story, you can see that more often than not, you might have made some of the same choices if you'd lived their life instead of yours."

Fox wasn't suggesting that you have to believe the person you disagree with is a "good guy." She was offering that it's helpful to understand how that person views themselves. She was talking about being interested in the culture and events and relationships that have formed that person's opinions, and considering how your thinking might be impacted if you'd been exposed to the same mixture of experiences.

She was also talking about checking your bias. Putting yourself in someone else's shoes is one way to do that. Another is to resist the impulse—and it is a strong one—to constantly decide whether you agree with everything someone says. *Listening* to someone doesn't mean agreeing with them. The purpose of listening is to understand, not to endorse.

Often, we decide very quickly whether or not we will agree with someone. We listen for certain words that might be clues to their politics or faith and we use them to categorize people into groups. Into one group, we gather all of the people who think like we do; and into the other go all of those who think differently. The problem is, these kinds of groupings are not very accurate.

Imagine your child wants to sleep over at a friend's house. You call up the friend's mom to chat about details. You want to make sure you trust her with your child's safety. You might have a nice conversation about local events, the weather, the news. But will you ask her about her house rules or her views on discipline? After all, just because you agree on climate change doesn't mean you agree on child rearing. Using political or social values as a standard for someone's family values could have unintended and even dangerous consequences.

This tendency to lump people into groups is known as the "halo and horns effect." Psychologists call it a cognitive bias or a "bias blind spot." Basically, when we approve of a single aspect of another person, we are more likely to judge them positively for other aspects. It takes just one common, important interest for us to find someone believable, trustworthy, and likeable.

The opposite is true as well: if we disapprove of someone's appearance, opinion, occupation, or another personal aspect, we are more likely to disapprove of everything about them. Like me, you must see this play out all the time in both public and private life. You hear that someone served time for drug possession and you make up your mind that they're threatening or untrustworthy. You hear that a friend's husband cheated on her, and you find you can't give him a good reference for a job.

Research suggests that while most of us acknowledge that bias exists, we don't think *we* are influenced by bias all that often. We accept the existence and pervasiveness of unconscious bias but aren't conscious of our own.

Here's the bald truth: we are all biased. Every human being is affected by unconscious biases that lead us to make incorrect assumptions about other people.[3] Everyone.

To a certain extent, bias is a necessary survival skill. If you're an early human, perhaps *Homo erectus*, wandering the jungles, you may see an animal approaching. You have to make very fast assumptions about whether that animal is safe or not, based solely on its appearance. The same is true of other humans. You make split-second decisions about threats in order to have plenty of time to flee, if necessary. This could be one root of our tendency to categorize and label others based on their looks and their clothes.

Decades ago, some psychologists thought prejudice was an unfortunate side effect of bad parenting. We now know that it's based both in survival instinct and in our need to make sense of a complicated world.[4] Racism is never acceptable, of course, but if we hope to eradicate it, we must understand its roots. And we must acknowledge that some of those roots, though not all, have biographical underpinnings. Prejudice against a race begins when we make stereotypes about that race: this person is bad and, therefore, all members of that race are bad.

A sense of community is important to humans and we are predisposed to think badly of anyone who is not a member of our group. We stereotype outsiders by lumping them into categories. According to Dr. John Bargh, a professor of psychology at Yale University, where he serves as the director of the Automaticity in Cognition, Motivation, and Evaluation (ACME) lab, "stereotypes are categories that have gone too far. When we use stereotypes, we take in the gender, the age, the color of the skin of the person before us, and our minds respond with messages that say hostile, stupid, slow, weak. Those qualities aren't out there in the environment. They don't reflect reality."

It might be tempting to believe that all stereotypes are rooted in history and ignorance, but some are actually quite modern and new ones arise regularly. In fact, scientists have been able to reproduce the creation of stereotypes in their labs, which means we are capable of creating new stereotypes at any time, and the passage of time will not serve to destroy them.[5] Stereotypes change and evolve over the years, which underscores an important fact about them: they are not based on fact or truth, but presumption. For example, it wasn't all that long ago that pink was considered a masculine color. A June 1918 issue of *Ladies Home Journal* advised parents that "the generally accepted rule is pink for the boys, and blue for the girls. The reason is that pink, being a more decided and stronger color, is more suitable for the boy, while blue, which is more delicate and dainty, is pretty for the girl."

Obviously, the opposite gender stereotypes prevail today. While the color of a baby blanket may seem like a frivolous example of stereotyping, its very silliness shows us how flimsy stereotypes are. When we enter a conversation, all of our preconceived notions—most of which have no basis in reality—will affect its outcome. No matter how right and true your opinion feels, consider that it may be a stereotype and not fact. Try to acknowledge your bias and set it aside for the duration of the conversation. Do your best to listen without judgment and to stop yourself from making minute-by-minute decisions about what you agree with.

Remember that many of our divisions can be attributed

to our habit of classifying everyone who disagrees with us as an "outsider." And when we view others as different from us, we struggle to find ways to make ourselves understand. Sometimes we just give up. Vinson Cunningham, staff writer for the *New Yorker*, wrote in a 2016 article that "the incredible danger of our polarization lies, I think, in a fact that has become unavoidably clear in recent months: the old common American language has all but evaporated, perhaps permanently . . . we speak no longer within one language (where understanding is hard, but possible) but across the gulf that seems, every day, to widen."[6] Acknowledging our bias can help to bridge the gap.

My third suggestion is to show respect at all times. In my opinion, respect is the cornerstone of any meaningful exchange of ideas. And a recent poll[7] suggests that many people agree with me on that point. Just about all of those polled said being respectful is even more important in conversations than finding common ground.

In order to show respect, you'll have to view the other person as a human being, deserving of respect. And you'll need to find a way to empathize with them, in spite of your disagreements. One way to do this is to assume that everyone is trying to bring about some kind of positive result in their lives. When you encounter someone you don't like or don't understand, try to identify what that goal is.

You can practice your empathy skills by watching a video of a public figure you don't agree with. Watch a speech given by that person or an interview they've done, and focus on seeing that person as someone trying to accomplish something they believe to be good. From their point of view, their end goal is positive and constructive. Try to imagine what that end goal is. Focus on their positive intentions. It's not easy, is it? But it's absolutely essential if you want to respect that person. Perhaps they have made different decisions than you have, perhaps they've learned different lessons, but in their mind, they are doing their best.

I try to practice my empathy skills in the car, which, for me, is very challenging. If someone cuts me off or runs a red light, my first instinct is to assume—and sometimes say aloud—terrible things about their intelligence and their upbringing. But what I've tried to do lately is imagine why they are in such a hurry or why they're in such a bad mood. Instead of the expletives that I *want* to say, I'll think, *She's probably had a bad day. Maybe she's just trying to get home to see her kid.* As a parent, I can empathize.

It doesn't really matter if my imagined scenario is

true or if the person is just a terrible driver, because the point of the exercise is to train my mind to see others as individuals who face daily challenges that are equal to mine. The point is to get into the habit of viewing others as fallible human beings who are just trying to make it in a very difficult world. The exercise benefits me, not the other person.

It is very difficult to have a productive conversation with someone you don't respect, and your opinion of them, and what they say, is not likely to be accurate.

My next piece of advice for navigating difficult conversations is to stick it out. If you're talking to someone and a taboo topic comes up—whether it's death, divorce, or race—don't try to change the subject. Don't make a joke or go off on a tangent. Conversations on tough issues are often uncomfortable, especially when you don't know what to say. But try to avoid getting frustrated and walking away. Silence is preferable to flight.

If you truly have nothing to say, then just listen. Accept that you may not reach an agreement and that disagreement is okay. Not every conversation, or even most, will end with a hug and an epiphany. Sometimes, just learning what someone else thinks, without changing any minds, is more than enough. Take joy in the exchange, or, at the least, take satisfaction.

And my final piece of advice really applies to all conversations but is especially true of difficult ones: end well. You don't need to have the last word. Let go of that impulse if you want to maintain friendly relations with the other person.

Also, take a moment to thank them for sharing their thoughts. It can be scary to talk about politics or religion with someone else, so express your gratitude for their time and their openness. If you end the conversation in a friendly and gracious way, you set the groundwork and the tone for future conversations.

Of course, you will not always follow these suggestions and that's all right. I don't expect you to be a perfect conversationalist, as I certainly am not. I once let an argument over police shootings get out of control to the point where my spouse and I slept in different rooms for a couple of days. Remember, emotion isn't a character flaw—we are hardwired as emotional creatures. Sometimes you'll succumb to the drama of the moment and your best intentions will go out the window.

If that happens and you say something you shouldn't, apologize immediately. Acknowledge that your comments were hurtful or wrong and make no excuses. Then you can put the mistake behind you and move forward.

If we can learn to talk about the hard things, if we

can find common ground and begin to discover the issues on which we can agree, it could be possible to solve some of the more intransigent problems we face. I encourage you to open your mind and your mouth and ask some new people new questions. It only takes one good conversation to change your understanding of someone else's world, your world, and the world at large.

Sometimes a tough conversation spirals out of control— intentions or words are misunderstood, people become angry, feelings get hurt. There's only one way to move forward: someone has to say they're sorry.

Apologizing isn't easy. It can be painful and awkward, but that's the point. When we apologize, the other person sees us struggling, knows we feel uncomfortable, and their compassion response kicks in. Sincere apologies are powerful agents for reconciliation.

I have found that a heartfelt apology can work miracles in a conversation and I have, at times, apologized for things for which I was not responsible. I've sometimes thought I'd like to take an apology tour around the world. Not the Apology Tour Barack Obama was accused of undertaking, but a journey from city to city to tell people that I'm sorry for the hard things they've been through.

Here's an example. I was in an airport recently, reading a book called *Blood at the Root*, preparing for an interview with the author. The book is about the expulsion of all of the African Americans in Forsyth County, Georgia, in 1912. Armed whites in the county used threats, violence, and fire to drive every black citizen outside the borders, and the county remained all-white for at least seventy-five years.[8]

A blond woman sitting across from me asked about the book and we started talking. She tells me she grew up in an all-white town. She says she remembered when a Mexican family moved in and that people were awful to them. Cashiers at the grocery store wouldn't look at them or speak to them. They would just woodenly ring up their items and wait in silence for the family to pay.

The woman tells me her parents said terrible things about that family, things that she now realizes were racist and hateful and totally unfounded. But, she says, she doesn't understand why people blame her for what her parents did. "It's just as racist to assume that I'm racist," she says.

"Just because I want everyone to come to the US legally doesn't mean I'm racist," she continues. "I don't care what color the person is or where they come from,

I just think they should follow the law. People have said the most awful things to me."

At that point, I moved to sit in the seat next to her, looked her in the eye, and said, "I'm so sorry. I really am. I'm sorry that you've been made to feel like you can't express your opinion without being called names and I'm so sorry that people said terrible things to you."

Because I was watching for it, I saw the woman's shoulders relax. I saw the muscles around her eyes relax and I saw her mouth fall into a slight smile. "Thank you," she said. "Thanks for saying that. I just feel so awful. I feel like I can't say anything."

We ended up chatting for another twenty minutes or so before Delta began boarding my flight. As I stood to go, she thanked me again for listening to her and told me she now understood how her views might be offensive to some people. "I never thought about how I was saying it. I just thought about what was in my heart," she said. "I didn't hear it from the other side."

I think she walked away with a broader perspective on the issue, although I can't really say for sure. But I know that I came away with more empathy for her and those who share her views. I also felt the pleasure of having given a sincere apology and having witnessed its transformative power firsthand.

Apologies can come from anyone if they are both heartfelt and honest. After years of indigenous people demanding an apology from the Australian government for its past horrific treatment of them, the nation established May 26 as "National Sorry Day." That might sound like a woefully insufficient response to a long-standing, systemic assault, but it provides a platform each year for the government to acknowledge the harm they caused and apologize for it.

Apologies are magic. That's how I've come to see them, even though scientists have identified the real, non-magical effects that conciliatory gestures have in our brains. Michael McCullough, a professor of psychology at the University of Miami, has done ground-breaking work on apologies and forgiveness. He says people wrongly assume that humans are innately selfish and mean. "Humans need relationship partners," McCullough says, "so natural selection probably also gave us tools to help us restore important relationships after they have been damaged by conflict."[9]

When someone has been wronged, their brain experiences a state of chemically induced turmoil. That person may try for years to satisfactorily resolve an unresolved emotional conflict, even subconsciously. Michael McCullough runs the Evolution and Human

Behavior Laboratory at the University of Miami in Coral Gables, where he studies behaviors like revenge and self-control and gratitude. He can explain the purpose of apologies much better than I. Here's an excerpt of his interview on the NPR show *On Being*, with host Krista Tippett:

MR. McCULLOUGH: If you look at the brain of somebody who has just been harmed by someone—they've been ridiculed or harassed or insulted—we can put those people into technology that allows us to see what their brains are doing, right? So we can look at sort of what your brain looks like on revenge. It looks exactly like the brain of somebody who is thirsty and is just about to get a sweet drink to drink or somebody who's hungry who's about to get a piece of chocolate to eat.

TIPPETT: It's like the satisfaction of a craving?

MR. McCULLOUGH: It is exactly like that. It is literally a craving. What you see is high activation in the brain's reward system. . . . The desire for revenge does not come from some sick dark part of how our minds operate. It is a craving to solve a problem and accomplish a goal.[10]

Even if you don't believe someone has cause to feel wronged, it doesn't change the intensity of the emotion in that person's mind. They *crave* resolution and relief. You can give them at least a taste of that.

Three things happen when you apologize sincerely. First, you acknowledge someone's anger or sadness. You validate that they have reason to be angry or that their anger is real. This often disarms them. Research shows that, after the apology, they no longer see you as a threat or as someone who might again harm them. They drop their defensive posture. And finally, when you're successful, their brain prepares to forgive. They may even be able to move on from the source of injury entirely. Beverly Engel, a psychotherapist who specializes in trauma recovery, writes in her book *The Power of Apology*, "While an apology cannot undo harmful past actions, if done sincerely and effectively, it can undo the negative effects of those actions."[11]

An apology can also confer upon the person offering it tremendous positive effects. In order to apologize to someone, you must first understand why they're upset. That requires that you put yourself in their shoes for just a moment, and we know that such an exercise increases empathy.

In order for me to apologize to the woman in the airport, I had to imagine what it felt like to her to be called a racist. She was obviously very hurt by that word. What was it like to feel unjustly insulted? While I listened to her and encouraged her to continue explaining her perspective, I tried to see it all through her eyes. I'm a better person for having done that, and it was not difficult at all for me to say to her, sincerely, "I'm sorry. I can see that must be hurtful and I'm sorry."

Let me emphasize that we're not talking about extreme circumstances here, but the average conversation you may have on a daily basis. I'm not suggesting you apologize to a murderer or anyone else who's committed an act of terrible cruelty. I'm not talking about a conversation with Pol Pot, I'm talking about a chat with a stranger in the coffee shop or a coworker in the lunchroom.

In the end, it really didn't matter if I agreed with the woman in the airport or not. What mattered is that I acknowledged her pain and allowed her the opportunity to speak about it. She dropped her defensive armor and listened with an open mind for what she said was the first time in her life, and she walked away feeling understood instead of angry. Perhaps she'll be more open to similar conversations in the future.

All of that because she struck up a conversation with a stranger who offered the apology she'd been seeking for decades. With all due respect to science—that sure seems like a little bit of magic to me.

THE POWER OF AN APOLOGY

On December 7, 1970, the chancellor of Germany, Willy Brandt, was on a state visit to Poland. At that point, Germany was in tense negotiations with its neighbor to the northwest. Brandt made a planned stop at a monument to the Warsaw Ghetto Uprising. It was a formal and somewhat stilted affair, not much different from any other state visit to a monument, except that Brandt was the leader of Germany and he was visiting a memorial to the site where thirteen thousand Jews had died at the hands of German soldiers.

In 1943, Poland was occupied by Germans. The nation had more than three million Jews living there when the Nazis invaded in the fall of 1939. The Germans crowded most of the Polish Jews into ghettos, where they died in large numbers from starvation and disease. The largest of those ghettos was in Warsaw. Up to four hundred thousand people were packed into two square miles.

During the summer of 1942, the Germans started removing thousands of Jews every day for "resettlement to the East." When the leader of the Jewish Council found out what "resettlement" meant, he took his own life. By the end of the year, the people in the ghetto realized that their friends and loved ones were not being taken to labor camps but were being led to their deaths. They decided to fight back.

Beginning in January 1943, the Jews of the Warsaw Ghetto fought the SS troops with guns and grenades. By April, they were ordered to surrender. They refused. So German soldiers moved methodically through the streets, lighting the homes and businesses of the Jews with flame-throwers. One survivor described it to the BBC: "The sea of flames flooded houses and courtyards. . . . There was no air, only black, choking smoke and heavy burning heat radiating from the red-hot walls, from the glowing stone stairs."[12]

In the end, thirteen thousand Jews died. Half of them succumbed to the flames or suffocation. The rest were killed by explosives, gunfire, and other violent means. The German commander, Jürgen Stroop, described it years later to his cellmate in a Polish jail: "What a marvelous sight it was. A fantastic piece of theater. My staff and I stood at a distance. I held the electrical device which would detonate all the charges simultaneously. Jesuiter called for silence. I glanced over at my brave officers and men, tired and dirty, silhouetted against the glow of the burning buildings. After prolonging the suspense for a moment, I shouted: Heil Hitler and pressed the button."[13]

I tell you this history so you can understand the significance of the visit by the leader of Germany to that memorial at the site where so many Jews were burned alive. The chancellor, by the way, had no hand in what happened in Warsaw. Brandt fled Germany in the 1930s to escape prosecution at the hands of the Nazis. He worked against Hitler's regime for years and had his German citizenship revoked. Brandt did not harm any Jews during the war.

In the video of the visit, you see Chancellor Brandt, stone-faced, dressed in a dark suit and overcoat, surrounded by officials and soldiers at attention, walking very slowly to the monument. When Brandt reaches the statue, he places a wreath of flowers in front of it and then, to the shock and surprise of everyone watching, he falls to his knees. He remained there for some time, in complete silence, kneeling with his hands clasped in front of him. All reports say the gesture was completely spontaneous and Brandt was simply overcome with the emotion of the moment. He signed the Treaty of Warsaw that day, which established Germany's new borders with Poland.

That simple act—kneeling in humble grief—was widely seen as a major breakthrough in relations between Germany and not just Poland but all of Eastern Europe. Brandt went on to receive the Nobel Peace Prize the following year and Poland erected a statue in his honor not far from the monument where he knelt in silence.

PART II

"My idea of good company . . . is the company of clever, well-informed people, who have a great deal of conversation; that is what I call good company."

"You are mistaken," said he gently, "that is not good company, that is the best."

—JANE AUSTEN, *PERSUASION*

The following ten chapters focus on the specific strategies I've identified that can immediately improve the conversations you have every day. When I say "immediately," I don't mean that you will suddenly become a master of conversation after putting down this book. In many cases, implementing these tools will require you to unlearn a lifetime of bad conversational habits. And that can take some time.

I've practiced these techniques for years now and I'm still getting a handle on them. Dropping bad habits is difficult. I encourage you to be patient with yourself. Choose one simple thing to work on first—it's a good idea to start with the area you think will be easiest to master. Do you have trouble remaining present in conversations? Do you get bored or distracted easily? Are you frequently tempted to multitask? Then turn to Chapter Six and work on improving your attention. Once you feel you can stay focused on conversations, you can move on to working on a different skill. The point is, take it one step at a time.

I want to establish from the outset that for the purposes of this book, when I reference "conversation" I am always talking about good conversation. Most of the exchanges that make up your day don't fall under that category, to my mind. We all have brief, specific conversations at work and at home that don't require nuance or patience. You don't have to worry about the kinds of questions you're asking if you're just talking about what movie you want to see or telling a coworker how to log in to their e-mail account.

This book is aimed at the conversations that are more complicated than that and, therefore, more prone to go wrong. If you try to turn every conversation into a deep, probing exchange, you'll be exhausted all the time. Let context dictate how you use what you learn here. If you're training someone, then it's totally okay to do most of the talking. If you're teaching them, then it's expected that you will try to educate them, even though I generally advise against doing that.

Also, I often turn to my own interviews as examples of how to implement these strategies. That's because my studies in conversation began as a way to become a better interviewer. You might think these examples don't apply to you because an interview is not a conversation. But, at its heart, that's exactly what an interview is.

Over the course of my research, the biggest surprise to me was that the techniques that helped me in the studio worked just as well in the coffee shop. These methods will help you in your office and your gym and your kid's school. They will also help if you happen to do a lot of interviews as a journalist or a recruiter. The advantage you have over me is that you most likely don't have to cut your conversations short because it's time to take a station break.

One further thing to remember: every conversation you have will be different from every other conversation you've ever had. I can't give you specific words to use or phrases to repeat that will make your conversations better. There's no such thing as a conversational skeleton key.

However, I have found that the best conversations occur when I am fully and authentically engaged. For example, I recently had a conversation with a colleague about updates to our studio. He began to detail the specifics of equipment pricing and shipment dates, and my mind started to wander. I responded by saying, "Whoa! Maybe I didn't have enough coffee, but I'm struggling to follow you. Can we go back to the part about when the equipment will be installed? That's probably as deep as my mind can go at the moment."

That worked for me. He laughed, I laughed, and then the conversation got back on track. But that probably won't work for you because that's not how you'd say it. My hope is that you will respond honestly and authentically in your conversations because that makes for the best exchanges.

One last thing before we get into the rules. Remember,

there are always exceptions to these rules. There are situations in which it's useful to offer a story about your experience for comparison. There are instances in which it's all right to ask complicated questions or talk about names and dates and other "weedy" details. There are times when interjecting your unrelated story about a funny thing that happened at the post office is exactly the right thing to do.

This book is the culmination of five years of research. I set out to collect the best information I could from the people who've studied these issues in depth and added insight from my own professional experience. Your observations are the third part of that triangle. It's important to consider your own experience, but I would caution against letting it override the bulk of professional opinion. (After you've read Chapter Seven, and learned just how easily the mind can be duped, you may understand why I recommend multiple layers of verification.)

I have found that following this advice leads to better conversations, deeper connections, and richer relationships. I hope it has the same impact in your life.

6

BE THERE OR GO ELSEWHERE

Everyone knows what attention is. It is the taking possession by the mind, in clear and vivid form, of one out of what seem several simultaneously possible objects or trains of thought.

—WILLIAM JAMES

If you think that you can efficiently do two things at once, you are wrong, I'm sorry to say. Contrary to popular belief, human beings aren't capable of multitasking.[1]

The concept of multitasking was never actually intended to apply to people. It was originally used to describe a computer that runs multiple programs at the same time. But the human brain doesn't work like a computer operating system. We can only focus on one thing at a time.

I know that many people *think* they can multitask, and I used to be one of them. If you've ever watched a short-order cook or an emergency room nurse or a middle school teacher work, you might be tempted to believe it's possible. But as MIT neuroscientist Earl Miller says, "The brain is very good at deluding itself."[2] When we think we're multitasking, what we're really doing is rapidly switching from one task to another. We don't perceive this shift in attention, so we believe that we can actually focus on two things at the same time. Sadly, that's why so many people continue to text while driving.

We can't do two things at once and that's especially true if those two things use the same part of the brain. That means we can't type an e-mail and talk on the phone at the same time because our left hemisphere can't juggle both tasks. According to Miller, "They both involve communicating via speech or the written word, and so there's a lot of conflict between the two of them." This conflict is known as interference.

The same holds true if you're having a conversation with a colleague while scrolling through your Facebook feed or talking to your auto mechanic while checking prices of transmissions on your tablet. I can't even begin to count the number of dishes I've burned because I was talking to my son and watching a movie while I cooked.

And yet, *trying* to multitask is very enjoyable to the

brain. That rapid switching from action to action "creates a dopamine-addiction feedback loop, effectively rewarding the brain for losing focus and for constantly searching for external stimulation," according to neuroscientist Daniel J. Levitin. In the end, we pay a high price for that dopamine rush. The rapid-fire switching in our neurons also increases the production of cortisol and adrenaline, two hormones that "can overstimulate your brain and cause mental fog or scrambled thinking."[3]

That means that while multitasking makes you feel superefficient, your thinking is actually clouded and you're likely not aware of the impact on your cognitive abilities. What's more, cortisol and adrenaline also cause feelings of stress and anxiety. So, we're pumped up while we're trying to do three things at once, but, after it's over, we're left feeling jittery. And, because our cognitive abilities were reduced, chances are we have good reason to feel nervous—we probably mucked up something along the way.

Therefore, if you want to have a good conversation, you must give it your full attention. I know how difficult this is, as our society values multitasking and we are surrounded by distractions. How many tabs do you normally keep open in your Internet browser? How many electronic devices do you now leave the house with? Just your smartphone? A smartphone and a tablet? If you're called into a meeting, what do you bring with you? We had an impromptu meeting at my office recently and I watched a colleague walk in carrying a laptop, smartphone, and tablet. She set up them all carefully as the meeting began and then paused for a moment to check the Fitbit on her wrist.

These devices give us the illusion of increased control and competency. They also make us feel as though we're highly informed. This technology makes us smarter, right? Brace yourself, because the facts don't bear out that little illusion, either. Psychologist Glenn Wilson found that if you are trying to focus on a task but you know that an unread e-mail is sitting in your in-box, your IQ can fall by 10 points. The prefrontal cortex, the part of the brain that helps us prioritize tasks and make executive decisions, is easily distracted by new stuff. It wants to look and see what the e-mail says. It expends energy thinking about opening that e-mail and your cognitive abilities drop.

Text messages may have an even bigger impact than e-mail because they don't have to be opened. Many phones display texts immediately, on top of whatever else you're looking at. "Add to that the social expectation that an unanswered text feels insulting to the sender," Daniel J. Levitin writes in the *Guardian*, "and you've got a recipe for addiction: you receive a text, and that activates your novelty centres. You respond and feel rewarded for having completed a task (even though that task was entirely unknown to you 15 seconds earlier). Each of those delivers a shot of dopamine as your limbic system cries out 'More! More! Give me more!'"[4]

Don't forget that each text you read also delivers a shot of cortisol and adrenaline, which fog your thinking and leave your system saying, "I'm so stressed! I'm so anxious!" The whole cycle is a recipe for bad work and bad feelings.

I know it feels like we're maximizing our time when we try to focus on multiple things. Technology entrepreneur M. G. Siegler defended this behavior in an essay titled "I Will Check My Phone at Dinner and You Will Deal with It," published on *TechCrunch*. "Forgive me, but it's Dinner 2.0," he writes. "And again, I'm having more fun at these dinners than I ever have. Is part of it antisocial? Sure. Can it lead to distractions if you read a work-related email that you need to respond to? Of course. But this is the way the world works now. We're always connected and always on call. And some of us prefer it that way."[5]

I can only surmise that the dopamine rush neuroscientists talk about is part of the reason "some of us prefer it that way," and I'm certainly not here to tell you what to do or shame you for the decisions you make. It would be hypocritical of me to do so, since I spent the better part of my adult life claiming to be a fantastic multitasker. For years, I even listed it on my résumé as a "special skill."

As happens with so many other things in life, I only learned my lesson after making mistakes. Most journalists work on several stories simultaneously. At any one time, I was juggling five to ten stories. For any one story, I would place dozens of calls to potential sources. That means I was answering calls, doing interviews, and taking notes during conversations with up to a hundred people over the course of a week.

It was probably inevitable that, while trying to multitask my way through such a large number of stories, I would make a mistake. Spoiler: I did. I was working on a story about the band Barenaked Ladies writing music for a production of Shakespeare's *As You Like It*. While editing audio, I was also interviewing sources for a story on the Chrysler Corporation, and writing a piece on race riots in Detroit. In the midst of all of that, I got something very wrong.

After the story on Barenaked Ladies aired on *Morning*

Edition, I got an e-mail from one of the professors that I'd spoken to. He said the quote in my report was very smart and he was gratified to be mentioned, but those words weren't actually his.[6] Calling my editor to admit that blunder was really difficult. That kind of mistake is a huge no-no for reporters; our reputation is built on our accuracy.

From that point on, I stopped juggling stories. If I had to answer the phone, I turned away from the computer and focused on the call. If I was writing, I turned the phone off, closed the door, and did nothing else except write. I may have been missing the dopamine, but the quality of my writing improved and, frankly, so did the quality of my conversations with sources.

So, I'm not here to make you feel guilty, just to help you learn what I learned the hard way. If good conversation is your goal, reading texts and e-mails while you're talking is a terrible idea. So much of conversation is nuance and subtlety. Checking in every ten seconds while you read your Twitter feed will ultimately result in missed messages and misunderstandings.

What's more, it's highly unlikely that you will retain what you've just heard unless you're focused. We have trouble remembering things we're told under the best circumstances. Multiple studies have demonstrated this. Research at the University of Minnesota showed that, even when people were instructed to listen closely, they could only recall about 50 percent of what they were just told. After two months, they could only recall about a quarter of what they'd listened to carefully. Those who watched the evening news for another study could remember less than 20 percent of what was said.[7]

Those same studies demonstrate that if a person doesn't listen carefully and closely, they forget up to half of the information they hear within eight hours. So, it's no surprise that something we tell our spouses while they're watching *Law & Order* won't stay with them, or that telling your kid to take out the trash while he or she is playing a video game and talking on the phone is equivalent to shouting it into an empty room. You may also want to rethink those annual all-staff meetings in which you discuss important issues. Chances are, you'll have to say the same things every year.

The point is, if you're not fully invested in a conversation, there's really no point in having it. I'm not talking about just putting down your phone or turning away from your computer. I'm talking about being *present*. The conversation will be just fine if you don't check your phone to see who starred in *The Maltese Falcon* (Humphrey Bogart) or who was president in 1974 (Nixon or Ford, depending on the month).

If you want to get out of a conversation, get out of it. Tell the other person, politely, that you have too much on your mind to really listen to what they're saying. "I need to gather my thoughts," I often say. "I'm so sorry, but I'm struggling to stay focused and I do want to hear what you have to say. Can I check back in later?"

You must commit to a conversation, even the brief ones, or walk away. If you're too distracted, admit that to both yourself and the other person. Be present or be gone.

The best, most effective method for learning to be present in conversation is meditation. Maybe you saw this one coming. Maybe you're rolling your eyes. For some reason, many people are put off by the prospect of meditating. I've never entirely understood why, but the two most common answers I've heard from people I know are that they don't have the time or that they associate meditation with religious practice.

While meditation is often associated with Buddhism, it is no more a religious ritual than practicing yoga. Much like yoga, meditation is a method. It's an exercise used to train the brain. We go to the gym to train our muscles; we use meditation to train our minds.

Mindfulness meditation teaches you how to be aware of your body, your breathing, and your thoughts. It does not require a lot of time. In fact, you can see benefits even if you only do it for five minutes a day. Some practitioners suggest you start with just a couple of minutes a day.

Research into the specific benefits of meditation is ongoing. We're not sure how much it helps alleviate depression or pain, for example. But multiple studies show that meditation improves stress levels and mood, and one study by a Harvard neuroscientist showed it might even increase gray matter in the frontal cortex, the area of the brain that's associated with memory and executive decision-making. In that study, benefits were measurable in a magnetic resonance imaging (MRI) scan after meditating forty minutes a day for eight weeks.[8]

You don't need forty minutes if you don't have the time, though. You can see benefits quickly, no matter how long you choose to meditate. And you don't need a teacher or a special app or soft music or soft lighting.

BECOMING MINDFUL

Meditating is simple: sit quietly, close your eyes, and focus on your breathing, while you allow thoughts to pass through your mind without dwelling on them. A thought comes and you notice it and then you let it go, while you return your focus to your breathing. You can count the breaths if you like, but you don't have to. And that's it! That's all that meditation is, at its simplest.

While it may be simple, it's not easy. It takes some time to get good at it. Buddha sat under his tree for seven days without moving. It's said he only got up because he was really, really hungry.

The point is, learning to let thoughts pass in and out of your mind is difficult. The brain is going to get distracted; that's a guarantee. You can't stop your brain from thinking. But you can train it not to follow every random thought that comes into your head. Meditation simply makes you aware of what the brain is thinking and gives you more control over which thoughts you dwell on and which you choose to release.

If you continue to practice meditation and you become more aware of what you're thinking, it might mean you're a slower talker. You might naturally pause more often to take note of what you're thinking. I see that as a positive.

Meditation will also benefit your conversation skills by making you a better listener. Once the chatter in your mind quiets down, you can really focus on what someone else is saying without becoming overly distracted by your own thoughts. And there are other benefits as well. For example, those who practice mindfulness meditation are less likely to burn out at work. They also tend to better cope with stress. That's a pretty good deal just for sitting quietly and breathing for a few minutes a day.

There are many variations on the simple formula I laid out. There's some very hopeful research into what's called loving-kindness meditation. I know that sounds like a class taught by a spiritual adviser who wears wooden beads and smells of patchouli, but it's an effective tool used by psychologists and physicians.

Loving-kindness meditation, or LKM, can reduce symptoms of depression and even decrease the severity of chronic pain. Just as important, it seems to have an impact on your emotional health and thought processes. People who practice LKM have more positive emotions than those who don't. It has been shown to decrease bias and foster empathy.

Here's how you practice LKM, in a nutshell. You send compassionate thoughts to yourself and to other people, and you breathe. You can do that in any method that you choose, but here is a common format:

1. Send compassionate thoughts to yourself.
2. Send them to someone you love.
3. Send them to a stranger.

4. Send them to someone you dislike or with whom you are currently in conflict.

5. Finally, send compassionate thoughts to all living beings.

This morning, I sent compassionate thoughts to myself, to my son, to the girl at the coffee shop with the great Scottish accent, to a person who will remain unnamed, and to the world. It took ten minutes.

As far as I know, meditation is the only effective way to train yourself to be present despite all the distractions of daily life. Meditation is, after all, a method to become more mindful. Whatever method you choose, the important thing is that you find a way to be mentally present in your conversations. Hear someone else's words and consider them; pay attention to both the spoken message and the unspoken. Be there or be gone.

7

IT'S NOT THE SAME!

Humans aren't as good as we should be in our capacity to empathize with feelings and thoughts of others, be they humans or other animals on Earth. So maybe part of our formal education should be training in empathy. Imagine how different the world would be if, in fact, that were "reading, writing, arithmetic, empathy."

—NEIL DEGRASSE TYSON

A good friend of mine lost her dad some years back. I found her sitting alone on a bench outside our workplace, not moving, just staring at the horizon. She was absolutely distraught and I didn't know what to say to her. It's so easy to say the wrong thing to someone who is grieving and vulnerable. So, I started talking about how I grew up without a father. I told her that my dad had drowned in a submarine when I was only nine months old and I'd always mourned his loss, even though I'd never known him. I just wanted her to realize that she wasn't alone, that I'd been through something similar and could understand how she felt.

But after I related this story, my friend looked at me and snapped, "Okay, Celeste, you win. You never had a dad and I at least got to spend thirty years with mine. You had it worse. I guess I shouldn't be so upset that my dad just died."

I was stunned and mortified. My immediate reaction was to plead my case. "No, no, no," I said, "that's not what I'm saying at all. I just meant that I know how you feel." And she answered, "No, Celeste, you don't. You have no idea how I feel."

She walked away and I stood there helplessly, watching her go and feeling like a jerk. I had totally failed my friend. I had wanted to comfort her and, instead, I'd made her feel worse. At that point, I still felt she misunderstood me. I thought she was in a fragile state and had lashed out at me unfairly when I was only trying to help.

But the truth is, she didn't misunderstand me at all. She understood what was happening perhaps better than I did. When she began to share her raw emotions, I felt uncomfortable. I didn't know what to say, so I defaulted to a subject with which I *was* comfortable: myself.

I may have been trying to empathize, at least on a conscious level, but what I really did was draw focus away from her anguish and turn the attention to me. She wanted to talk to me about her father, to tell me about the kind of man he was. She wanted to share her cherished memories of him so I could fully appreciate the magnitude of her loss. Instead, I asked her to stop for a moment and listen to my story about my dad's tragic death.

From that day forward, I started to notice how often I responded to stories of loss and struggle with stories of my own experiences. My son would tell me about clashing with a kid in Boy Scouts and I would talk about a girl I fell out with in college. When a coworker got laid off, I told her about how much I struggled to find a job after I had been laid off years earlier. But when I began to pay a little more attention to how people responded to my attempts to empathize, I realized the effect of sharing my experiences was never as I intended. What all of these people needed was for me to hear them and acknowledge what they were going through. Instead, I forced them to listen to me and acknowledge me.

Sociologist Charles Derber describes this tendency to insert oneself into a conversation as "conversational narcissism." It's the desire to take over a conversation, to do most of the talking, and to turn the focus of the exchange to yourself. It is often subtle and unconscious.[1]

Derber writes that conversational narcissism "is the

key manifestation of the dominant attention-getting psychology in America. It occurs in informal conversations among friends, family, and coworkers. The profusion of popular literature about listening and the etiquette of managing those who talk constantly about themselves suggests its pervasiveness in everyday life."

Derber describes two kinds of responses in conversations: a shift response and a support response. The first shifts attention back to yourself and the second supports the other person's comment. Here is a simple illustration:

Shift Response
MARY: I'm so busy right now.
TIM: Me, too. I'm totally overwhelmed.

Support Response
MARY: I'm so busy right now.
TIM: Why? What do you have to get done?

Here's another example:

Shift Response
KAREN: I need new shoes.
MARK: Me, too. These things are falling apart.

Support Response

KAREN: I need new shoes.

MARK: Oh yeah? What kind are you thinking about?

Shift responses are a hallmark of conversational narcissism. They help you turn the focus constantly back to yourself. But a support response encourages the other person to continue their story. It lets them know you're listening and interested in hearing more.

The game of catch is often used as a metaphor for conversation. Ideally, a conversation is a constant exchange of attention and focus. It's active because there is a continuous shift between talking about what's on your own mind and focusing on what someone else is saying. (Perhaps a more fitting twenty-first-century analogy would be a perpetual switch on your camera phone between selfie mode and portrait mode: focused on me, focused on them, focused on me, focused on them.) That's why the comparison to playing catch is so apt.

In an actual game of catch, you're forced to take turns. In conversation, we often find ways to resist giving someone else a turn. Sometimes we use passive means to subtly grab control of the exchange. Here's an example, based on Derber's research:

JOSH: I saw that new movie last night!

DAN: Oh.

JOSH: It was great. I really enjoyed it.

DAN: Nice.

JOSH: Have you seen it yet?

DAN: Yeah, I didn't think it was good. I thought the acting was stilted and . . . [*goes into long analysis of the movie*].

In this case, Dan didn't respond with any energy until Josh gave up control and asked him a question. Dan may not have been conscious of the fact that he was forcing Josh to hand over the reins of the conversation. For many of us, taking control of an exchange is habitual.

The tug-of-war over attention is not always easy to track. We sometimes very craftily disguise our attempts to shift focus. We might start a sentence with a supportive comment and then follow up with a comment about ourselves. For example, if a friend tells us they just got a promotion, we might respond by saying, "That's great! Congratulations. I'm going to ask my boss for a promotion, too. I hope I get it."

Such a response could be perfectly fine, as long as we allow the focus to shift back to the other person again.

The healthy balance is lost when we repeatedly shine the attention back on ourselves. We're lobbing ball after ball at the other person, who may well want to duck and run.

While reciprocity is an important part of any meaningful conversation, the truth is that shifting the attention to our own experiences is, at its core, a completely natural instinct. Modern humans are hardwired to talk about themselves more than any other topic. Research shows that we spend about 60 percent of our time in conversations talking about ourselves. Most of the remaining time is spent talking about a third person, *not the person we're talking to*. One study found that "most social conversation time is devoted to statements about the speaker's own emotional experiences and/or relationships, or those of third parties not present."[2]

Part of this hardwiring lies in a neurological phenomenon known as convergent information. When someone tells us a story, our brain automatically scans our memory for a comparable experience. In her book *Being a Brain-Wise Therapist*, Bonnie Badenoch writes, "If I watch you lick an ice cream cone, the same neurons will fire in both our brains, even though I only get to lick the ice cream internally." The same principle holds true when we hear someone describe an experience—

the brain responds as if it's been presented with a visual stimulus.[3]

The insula, an area of the brain deep inside the cerebral cortex, takes in the information and then tries to find a relevant experience in our memory banks that can give context to the information. It's mostly a helpful process: the brain is trying to make sense of what we hear and see.

Subconsciously, we find similar experiences of our own, add them to what's happening at the moment, and then the whole package of information is sent to the limbic regions, the part of the brain just below the cerebrum. And that's where some trouble can arise. Instead of helping us better understand someone else's experience, our own experiences can distort our perceptions of what the other person is saying or experiencing.

For example, suppose your sister tells you a story about a delicious dinner she made. Immediately, your brain will begin to search for any comparable experiences you've had. Did she mention mushrooms? Your brain scans your memory for information about the flavor of mushrooms. Did she say she cut her finger? Your brain retrieves a memory of the time you had to go to the ER for stitches. Your brain then sends all the converging information to your body to analyze. Your mouth might salivate if you think mushrooms are delicious. Your finger might ache a tiny bit from remembered pain. All of that sensory experience comes back to the brain to be absorbed and integrated. It happens so rapidly and automatically that we are not usually aware of it.

When everything works properly, this biological response helps us feel empathy toward the other person. We can imagine how delicious that dinner was. We can imagine how painful it must have been to nick a finger with a sharp knife.

But sometimes things go wrong. What if your relevant experience doesn't fully match your sister's story? You've eaten beef Stroganoff with mushrooms, but it tasted awful. Your experience with a knife injury was more serious than hers. When your experiences don't match up, you replace the other person's evaluation ("it didn't hurt that much") with your own ("knives are really dangerous"). As behavior change specialist Judith Martens writes, "Most times, you try to understand someone else by relating his story to your own experiences. If this is all you do, you are seeing the other as if he *is you*. Guess what, he is not! Relating to your own experiences is *not* a good start for true understanding."[4]

This is a point on which I receive a lot of resistance.

Almost universally, people tell me that sharing similar experiences is a good way to show empathy. But in fact, research suggests otherwise. A study from the Max Planck Institute for Human Cognitive and Brain Sciences suggests that our egos distort our perception of our own empathy, so that we're not good judges of when we're being empathetic and when we're not.[5]

When participants in the study watched a video of maggots in a group setting, they could understand that other people might be repulsed by the video. But if one person was shown pictures of puppies while the other unfortunate people were shown the maggot video, the puppy viewer generally underestimated the rest of the group's negative reaction to the maggots. Study author Dr. Tania Singer observed, "The participants who were feeling good themselves assessed their partners' negative experiences as less severe than they actually were. In contrast, those who had just had an unpleasant experience assessed their partners' good experience less positively." In other words, we tend to use our own feelings and perceptions as a basis to determine how others feel.

Here's how that translates to your daily conversations: Let's say you and a friend are both laid off at the same time by the same company. In that case, using your own feelings as a measure of your friend's feelings may be fairly accurate because you're experiencing the same event.

But what if you're having a great day and you meet a friend who was just laid off? Without knowing it, you'll judge how your friend is feeling against the standard of your good mood. She'll say, "This is awful. I'm so worried that I feel sick to my stomach." And you might respond, "Don't worry, you'll be okay. I was laid off six years ago and everything turned out fine." The more comfortable you are, the more difficult it is to empathize with the suffering of another.

While empathy is innate in most humans, it is also limited and can be challenging to maintain under the best circumstances. Most of us have read about experiments in which people willingly caused pain to others in a laboratory setting. The most famous of these is the Milgram experiment, which took place in 1961 at Yale University. In this study, participants were told to press a button to deliver electric shocks of increasing intensity to a person in another room. The study subjects were unaware that the test wasn't real and that electric shocks were never really administered.

The highest setting on the button was marked "Danger: severe shock." And yet more than half of the participants pressed the button when told to do so—even when they could hear the person in the other room pleading for mercy. But we don't need a laboratory to prove that empathy can be subverted. We need look no farther than our own history to see many horrendous examples of cruelty and torture. It's not necessary, in this book, to delve deeply into those events.

As the Milgram experiment illustrates so vividly, outside factors can weaken our ability to feel empathy for another human being. But some of those factors might come as a surprise. For example, the amount of money in your bank account affects your empathy for other people. You might think the poorest among us, who are struggling to get by, would be the least able to identify with the feelings of others. You might imagine they'd be consumed with their own needs, which are pressing and sometimes dire. But you would be wrong.

It turns out, the more money you have, the less able you are to correctly identify other people's emotions. It doesn't matter if you're looking at photos or interacting with real people, if you're wealthy, you likely have a harder time recognizing joy, fear, love, and anxiety in a stranger's face. (You're also more likely to be rude in conversation, which I think is related to empathy.)[6]

In this case, income was the only differentiating factor. "It was across gender, across ethnic backgrounds," says the author of the study, Sara Konrath. Konrath says those with lower incomes showed "greater empathic accuracy in the study." While many people believe education can increase empathy, that may not be entirely true, either. In Konrath's extensive research, people with only a high school diploma scored 7 percent higher than those with a college degree.[7]

But here's the interesting part of that study, in my eyes. At one point, a group of students were told to imagine Bill Gates as the top of the socioeconomic ladder. (That doesn't require a lot of imagination. He is quite literally at the top of that ladder, with a net worth of $75 billion.) The students were asked to imagine where they were on the ladder in relation to Bill Gates at the top. Most of us rank fairly low compared to Gates, so this group was imagining themselves as doing far worse than another person.

Another group was told to imagine someone at the very bottom of the scale, someone with absolutely nothing. And then they were told to imagine their place somewhere above the destitute person. Most people are doing relatively well compared to a homeless person with no money or property, so they were thinking of themselves as being much better off than someone else.

After those exercises, the researchers tested for empathy. All of the participants were shown photographs of strangers and asked to identify the emotion they saw in the other person's eyes. (That's a common test for empathic accuracy: how well you identify another person's emotions.) Turns out, those who pictured themselves somewhere below Bill Gates on the wealth scale—those who had just imagined themselves doing far worse than someone else—were fairly accurate at identifying emotions. Those who compared themselves to a homeless person, and thought of themselves as far above another, scored significantly worse.

Nothing about their financial circumstances had changed. In other words, simply thinking of yourself as rich by comparison makes you less empathetic. Imagining that you are relatively poor does the opposite.

Let's pause for a moment and make sure we all understand the limitations of scientific research. It's important to note that all studies are limited in scope and meaning. This study, for example, focused on people at a university, so it didn't reach either the richest or the poorest members of our society. Scientists don't usually state anything conclusively until multiple studies have been done by various independent groups. Even after a number of studies have been done, however, social science research is still limited, as it is nearly impossible to reproduce real-world situations in a clinical setting. And yet, though it has limitations, this research is provocative and hopeful to me.

It's hopeful because it suggests that empathy can be learned and nurtured. Just thinking that others are doing far better than you are makes you more empathetic. As Sara Konrath explains, "There's more fluidity to [empathy] than previously thought." Your level of empathy can go down, of course, but it can also go up. *Compassion can be learned*. That's a crucial takeaway.

An area of the brain called the right supramarginal gyrus (RSG) controls this response. The RSG helps us feel empathy and overcome what scientists call "emotional egocentricity." The RSG recognizes when we are responding in a narcissistic way and often tries to correct our perception.

But the RSG is highly complicated and sensitive and is affected by a dizzying array of factors that can prevent it from working properly. Even a small thing like being pressed for time can prompt the RSG to focus on your own emotions instead of someone else's. And as I mentioned, the happier and more comfortable you are, the more work the RSG needs to do and the more likely it is that your emotions will distort your perception of the other person.

This is not always a bad thing. If you're in danger or trying to meet an important deadline, it's imperative that you focus on your own needs above another's. But if "emotional egocentricity" occurred only when it was needed, we wouldn't be talking about its negative effects on conversation.

The words people use to express themselves also influence how we perceive their emotions because we unconsciously add our own context and experience to the meaning of those words. Communications expert Robert Chen, who coaches top executives on "soft skills," says, "If you assumed that just because you speak English and the other person speaks English that you're both speaking the same language, you're very wrong. The meaning you give to words [is a product of] your environment and your experience with that word."

This is one reason why miscommunication occurs so often. You may think you and your conversation partner are talking about a similar experience, but the same words don't always describe the same experience.

It took me years to realize that I was much better at the game of catch than I was at its conversational equivalent. Now I try to be more aware of my instinct to share stories and talk about myself. I try to ask questions that encourage the other person to continue. I've also made a conscious effort to listen more and talk less.

Recently, I had a long conversation with a friend of

mine who was going through a divorce. We spent almost forty minutes on the phone and I barely said a word. At the end of our call, she said, "Thank you for your advice. You've really helped me work some things out." The truth is, I hadn't actually offered any advice; most of what I said was a version of "That sounds tough. I'm sorry this is happening to you." She didn't need advice or stories from me. She just needed to be heard.

As with anything, there are exceptions to this rule. I'm sure there will be conversations in which it's helpful for you to share your own experiences. But most of the time, refocusing the conversation on you is unlikely to be helpful and can actually be hurtful. What's more, it's never wrong to choose *not* to talk about yourself. As they say, the mouth shuts, the ears don't, and there's a good reason for that.

8

GET OFF THE SOAPBOX

I never give advice unless someone asks me for it. One thing I've learned, and possibly the only advice I have to give, is to not be that person giving out unsolicited advice based on your own personal experience.

—TAYLOR SWIFT

When I moved to Georgia in 2014, I became a Southerner for the first time in my life. I was raised in California and have lived in Arizona, Washington, Michigan, New Jersey, and Maryland, but I'd never put down stakes in the South. However, my family tree has its roots in the South. One of my ancestors was a slave on a Georgia plantation in Milledgeville, a small town northeast of Macon, less than a two-hour drive from Atlanta.

If you read the biography of my great-grandmother in *The Encyclopedia of Arkansas History and Culture*, you'll see that her father's name is "unknown."[1] That may be the truth according to the official record, but our family knows who he was. He was the Scotch-Irish man who owned Anne Fambro, my great-great-grandmother. Carrie Lena Fambro was his daughter, born in 1872. When the era of legal slavery came to an end with the Civil War, he provided all of his mixed-race children, I'm told, with a college education.

Carrie got a degree from Atlanta University in 1886 and became a fierce advocate for the education of African Americans. She founded the first library for blacks in the Deep South, using funds raised by staging Shakespeare's plays. She taught at Union School, the first school for black children in Little Rock, Arkansas. These stories are part of my history; I've heard them retold many times and I've shared them with my own son.

I also grew up listening to stories about the ways my family has suffered because of racism. When my grandfather was to be awarded an honorary doctorate at Oberlin College, he decided to drive from Los Angeles to Ohio with his whole family. Unfortunately, they weren't allowed to stay at most hotels because he was black, and they couldn't stay at the black hotels because my grandmother was white. So, he drove nearly twenty-four hundred miles without stopping to get to Oberlin.

I'm quite light-skinned, yet I was the second-darkest

kid in my elementary school in Southern California. In third grade, one of the other kids called me a "nigger" and I punched him in the eye, without hesitation. I was sent to the principal's office and I still remember how scared I was outside his office. I was a good student and I didn't get in trouble very often. I knew my mother's reaction would be harsh if she had to pick me up from school. But the principal told me that if anyone else called me that word, I should punch them, too. And then he sent me back to class.

Needless to say, moving to Georgia was an emotionally turbulent experience for me. You can imagine my feelings when I discovered that, as a state employee, I got a day off for Robert E. Lee's birthday and another for Confederate Memorial Day. (The latter has since been renamed simply "State Holiday.") And you might be able to understand my reaction as I drove down the highway and saw the Confederate battle flag flying over people's homes.

And yet, when the debate over the battle flag reignited in the wake of the horrific massacre of nine people in the Emanuel African Methodist Episcopal Church in Charleston, South Carolina, my duty as a journalist was to cover the issue. We devoted an entire hour of my radio show to a discussion of that flag, its history and significance. We invited guests to join the debate who believed that the Confederate flag is a symbol of Southern identity and pride and that it should fly freely on government property as a tribute to the heroism of the soldiers who died defending the Confederacy.

I spent some time examining my own thoughts before that show. I knew there was no way that defenders of the flag could possibly understand my emotional reaction to it. They couldn't know my family's history or understand my personal experience. In turn, I had to acknowledge that I couldn't know their history or understand their experience.

I also wanted to be fair to my audience; they deserved to know about any bias I brought to the table. So, at the beginning of that show, I read the following disclaimer:

In the interest of full disclosure, I want to be clear about my perspective on this issue. I'm a mixed-race woman whose ancestors were slaves on a Georgia plantation. I can't pretend that I'm unbiased on the Confederate battle flag, as the flag is a symbol of torture, oppression, and enslavement to me.

However, I'm also a professional journalist and I welcome an open, honest conversation from all sides on the issue. I don't make public policy. My job is to give you all the information and let you decide as objectively as possible. . . . As always, we don't just welcome your comments, we'd love you to enter the conversation with us.

Those interviews were among the hardest I've done in my long career. Some of the things people said were personally hurtful and painful to hear. I was often tempted to argue or interrupt, but I remained professional and curious, and it paid off. I have since had great conversations with members of the Sons of Confederate Veterans. I don't agree with them on this issue, but I understand them better.

Our differing opinions *on this one issue* of the battle flag didn't interfere with our ability to talk to one another or respect one another, and it doesn't necessarily follow that because we disagree on this, we disagree on everything. Furthermore, our disagreements didn't prevent us from listening to one another. In order to have important conversations, you will sometimes have to check your opinions at the door. There is no belief so strong that it cannot be set aside temporarily in order to learn from someone who disagrees. Don't worry; your beliefs will still be there when you're done.

If you're like most people, you probably tend to avoid engaging in conversation with people you think are bigoted. We imagine that those who are less educated or less intelligent than we are probably don't have as enlightened a worldview.

But that would be your bias showing.

While we assume that smarts and education make us more open-minded than people less educated or intelligent, the truth is that research shows that the smarter you are, the *more* susceptible you are to bias. "If anything," the study reads, "a larger bias blind spot was associated with higher cognitive ability."[2]

This is all part of what's called unconscious or implicit bias. These are biases that affect our judgment but that we're unaware of and sometimes not even in control of. They are stereotypes, either positive or negative, of others that influence our views of them. Conscious biases are often choices we make about what we like or don't like: you prefer employees who dress professionally or you like waiters who call you "sir." Unconscious biases are harder to change because we often don't know we have them.

But maybe you're willing to accept that you have biases. You may think you're aware of your own prejudices and are actively working to eliminate them. That might be true on some level, but there's no evidence that people who are aware of their own biases are better able to overcome them than those who are unaware of their biases. And no matter how much thought you give to the issue, you're probably not aware of all the prejudices that influence your thinking. They're called unconscious biases for a reason, after all.

My point is, you may avoid a conversation with a racist, not realizing how hypocritical you are. You may be subject to just as many biases as the person you think you can't talk to. We all have these biases, regardless of race, gender, income, or religion.

Imagine how presumptuous it is to enter a conversation in order to educate someone else about their biases when you are unaware of your own. As a multiracial woman with light skin, I'm often in a unique position to observe other people's implicit bias. I once moderated a panel on the author James Baldwin with three African American professors. At one point, one of the panelists mentioned Barack Obama's "black heritage." I commented, "Remember that Obama is half white, so he has white heritage as well."

The panelist turned to the largely African American audience and pulled a face. Then he pointed to me and said, "Should I explain it to her?" I waited for the laughter to die down and then responded, "I'm multiracial, so I understand the need to balance both the white and the black cultures in a family." He jokingly yelled, "You dogged me!" I said, "Brother, you dogged yourself."

No one would argue that this acclaimed professor wasn't intelligent or educated, but biases affect us all. Schooling and smarts won't protect us from stereotyping.

The goal of an honest, respectful dialogue is to open our minds, not to change them. In fact, research suggests that changing our minds is a fiendishly difficult task.

In one study, researchers at Georgia State University and the University of Michigan gave study participants a series of fake news articles about a hot-button political topic. Then they gave the subjects an accurate article that explained what the previous articles got wrong. Imagine the surprise of the researchers when they found that reading the real news article only made people believe more strongly in the fake news they read first.

"Fake news" has been a common phrase since the 2016 election in the United States. People read that Pope Francis had endorsed Donald Trump (he didn't) and that "pizza" was a code word for a child sex trafficking ring run by members of Hillary Clinton's campaign (it wasn't). One of the dangers of "fake news" is that once someone has read it, it can become part of their belief system and very difficult to dislodge.

This phenomenon is called the backfire effect. When we learn we're wrong about something, we're often compelled to adhere more stubbornly to our original, incorrect belief. It's an unconscious process, so it's not as though anyone actually says, "I know I'm wrong, but I'm sticking with the lie." It's called the backfire effect because correcting inaccurate information can backfire and make a person stick even more adamantly to something that isn't true.

You might imagine that one solution to this problem is to do research so you can recognize untruths when you see them. But reading up on a subject doesn't seem to help. When we are very knowledgeable on a subject, we are often more likely to assume we know what's true and to accept information that supports our beliefs, even if it's false.

In his book *You Are Not So Smart*, journalist David McRaney writes about a study on differing views of the demonstrations that turned deadly at Kent State University in 1970, when National Guard soldiers shot and killed several protestors. "What is astonishing," McRaney said, "is they found the beliefs were stronger the more the participants said they knew about the event. The bias for the National Guard or the protesters was stronger the more knowledgeable the person was on the subject. The people who only had a basic understanding experienced a weak backfire effect when considering the evidence. The backfire effect pushed those who had put more thought into the matter farther from the gray areas."[3]

This is why conspiracy theories will persist no matter how much data is presented to refute them. It's why some people will always believe Obama is not an American citizen or astronauts never walked on the moon. And it's a very good reason why you shouldn't waste your time trying to disabuse someone of what you think is an incorrect opinion.

There is good news on this front, however. Further research into the backfire effect demonstrates that it might be rare and not nearly as widespread as initially believed. When two political scientists tried to re-create the backfire effect in a study, they found that participants were resistant to factual correction on only one subject: weapons of mass destruction (WMDs) in Iraq. On almost every other issue, the participants listened to and respected the factual information they were given. Perhaps we're not living in a "post-truth" world after all.

That said, it's important to note that participants in the study often held fast to the political ideologies and information that supported their side and discredited the opposing side. Study author Ethan Porter of George Washington University told the Poynter Institute for Media Studies that "there's still differential responsiveness, people still have their political beliefs. It's just that the picture may not be as dire as is commonly painted."[4]

It's nice to have some reassurance that political arguments can be grounded in fact. But why bother arguing about politics anyway? Have you ever gotten into an argument about a hot-button issue and heard the other person say, "You know what? You're right. I was wrong about that. Thank you so much for enlightening me." That has never happened to me. Not once.

Some arguments, however, can be productive if they're handled properly. Apple cofounder Steve Jobs famously thought arguments among his employees led to innovation. "Through that group of incredibly talented people bumping up against each other," he said, "having arguments, having fights sometimes, making some noise and working together, they polish each other [like rocks] and they polish the ideas."[5]

So, how do you handle an argument properly? For starters, if there's tension between you and another person, it's best to address it sooner rather than later. The tension often increases with the passage of time instead of dissipating.

Imagine this: You're at a theatrical performance and during a dramatic scene, the lead actress's wig starts to slide off her head. Probably the worst thing she can do at that point is to ignore the wig. No one in the audience will hear a word she says, no matter how great the dialogue is. They will be focused on that wig, waiting for it to drop.

A better solution would be to grab it and take it off, or fix it while saying, "This damn thing never stays on." She needs to openly acknowledge that something has gone wrong and then do her best to make it right. The same holds true for tension in a relationship: ignoring the problem doesn't make it go away.

Don't avoid a conversation because you're afraid of an argument. If the argument is coming, face it and try to make it as productive as possible. There are some simple ways to do this:

1. Don't make it personal. Don't talk about their personal flaws or use phrases like "This is what you always do" or "Here's your problem."
2. Think about solutions instead of focusing only on what you don't like or what made you angry. A productive argument isn't just a chance to complain.

3. Be willing to let the other person win. Finding a resolution that helps you both doesn't always mean declaring a victor or affirming that you are right.

Arguments happen when people's emotions are involved. There's nothing wrong with being passionate about a subject and being invested in its outcome. But passion can also lead to misunderstandings and hurt feelings, so I think the best conversations occur before an argument is necessary.

Any time you enter a conversation, and especially when you are about to talk with someone who holds different beliefs from your own, ask yourself: What do you hope to get out of this exchange? What would you like to have happen at the end and how would you like to walk away from the other person? Angry, frustrated, and no smarter than when you started? You probably cannot change their mind, so perhaps your goal should be your own enlightenment. You can't control what they take away from the conversation, but you can control what you get out of it.

As a journalist, I have had to learn how to open myself up in this way. It's not easy, and it takes training and a lot of practice. Often, you learn through your mistakes. The questions you didn't ask because you assumed you knew the answers, the people you didn't interview because you thought they had nothing valuable to add to the story. I've done practice interviews over and over while a coach pointed out the places where I'd stated my own opinion or shut someone down before they had the chance to express their views.

It starts with asking yourself some basic questions. No matter how strong your opinions are, dive into every topic thinking, "What if the other person is right? Why do they think the way they do?"

Unfortunately, research shows that many of us would rather avoid these conversations entirely. More than half of all Americans say most of their friends share their political views and we are really reluctant to talk about issues that might spark an argument.[6] Pew Research calls this the "spiral of silence." Most people (excluding online trolls) are not willing to share their views on politics, either on social media or in person, unless they are reasonably convinced that people agree with them.[7]

I think you can see the effects of this tendency all around us. Whether the issue is climate change, migrant refugees, abortion, or terrorism, we prefer to talk to people who share our opinions. We prefer to hear news that supports the opinions we already have. We choose to unfriend people who post things we don't like. We don't want to change our minds.

Not only is our information tailored to suit our opinions, but our personal relationships are as well. We may work with people whose opinions are vastly different from our own, we may see them almost every day, but unless we engage with them in an honest, civil dialogue, can we say that we really understand them? How can we solve complicated issues if we don't talk to the people right in front of us?

It's a problem that goes beyond our living rooms and offices. Congress has been remarkably unproductive in the past decade. In fact, the 112th Congress created only 284 laws, the fewest since 1973. And while politicians once crossed the aisle regularly to vote on bills, sometimes agreeing with their own party leaders and sometimes not, voting records now show a stark, clear divide, with most votes coming down to party lines. It is thought this change is partly caused by the drop in social interaction on Capitol Hill.

Democrats and Republicans used to attend the same parties, go out for lunch, meet for drinks. Their spouses used to know one another and their kids would go to one another's birthday parties. People on different sides of the aisle used to talk to each other. That rarely happens anymore.

As a nation, as a culture, as a functional society, we

are stagnating. We are separating the entire population into groups of us (those who agree with us) and them (those who don't). If you only speak to people who agree with you, you shut out the possibility of new perspectives, discoveries, and information.

I'm not suggesting you remain in conversation with someone who is spouting hateful rhetoric or subject yourself to abusive remarks. All I'm saying is, just because someone supports a candidate that you don't like, that doesn't mean you disagree with them on everything and can't find common ground. Just because someone has a strong opinion on taxes doesn't mean you won't connect on a shared experience of parenting or sports.

The famed therapist M. Scott Peck wrote that true listening *requires* a setting aside of self. "Sensing this acceptance, the speaker will feel less and less vulnerable and more and more inclined to open up the inner recess of his or her mind to the listener."[8]

This setting aside of the self—and all of the opinions, causes, beliefs, and biases that come with it—is one of the cornerstones of great conversation.

One of the best lessons I've learned in nearly twenty years as a journalist is that everyone has something to teach me. If you can find it within yourself to stop using conversations as a way to convince people that you're right, you will be stunned at what you've been missing. A flood of information will rush in to fill the vacancy left behind by your ego. You might be overwhelmed with knowledge, perspective, insight, and experience. You'll hear stories you had refused to hear because you were too busy stating and restating your case. If you enter every conversation assuming you have something to learn, you will never be disappointed.

If you want to articulate your opinion, write a blog. If you want to have a conversation, set your opinions aside, at least temporarily. You might find you never want to return to them. You may find you've evolved beyond them.

9

KEEP IT SHORT

One false word, one extra word, and somebody's
thinking about how they have to buy paper towels at
the store. Brevity is very important. If you're going
to be longwinded, it should be for a purpose. Not just
because you like your words.

—PATRICIA MARX

Did you know that most interviews on public radio are
only about five minutes long? They often seem longer
because they're packed with information, but they're actually quite brief. It takes longer to cook a frozen pizza
than it does for Steve Inskeep to interview Elizabeth
Warren about economic policy.

Your conversations will probably never be as concise
as an edited interview, but they don't have to be as long
and rambling as a Senate filibuster. Keeping conversations short is a discipline. It's not easy, but it's incredibly rewarding. If what you have to say is important and
you want people to remember it, then keep it short and
sweet.

The fact is, we can't pay attention for very long. As I mentioned in Chapter Two, attention spans have been on the decline for years and are now believed to be on par with those of goldfish (and actually, goldfish can pay attention for one second longer than modern humans can). When we are casually reading or surfing the Internet, the average person's attention span is just eight seconds long.

The results are a little better if we're focused on a task, but still not great. Researchers at the University of Michigan studied attention in a different way. They followed workers as they went about their business and reset stopwatches every time they changed tasks on the computer or switched to a new Web page. In 2004, when they first conducted the study, the average attention span was three minutes. In 2012, they tried it again and found the average had dropped to 1 minute 15 seconds. By 2014, it was down to 59.5 seconds.[1]

Most researchers blame this phenomenon on technology, and it's true that younger people are especially prone to getting bored. People between the ages of eighteen and twenty-four rarely give their full attention to any one thing for long. Nearly 80 percent use their smartphones or tablets while they are watching TV. They might believe they are multitasking, but we know that's an illusion.

The implications of our dwindling attention span are widespread. Our ability to focus relates to our health. (How long can we exercise? How much time can we spend in the kitchen cooking our own meals?) It also impacts our relationships. (How much patience do we have with others? Can we focus on what someone else is saying or doing?) Our attention span even impacts our IQ. Our intelligence may be determined not only by what we know but also by what our brain can ignore while it focuses on something else.[2]

But a short attention span isn't entirely bad. The report from the University of Michigan study concluded that "consumers are becoming better at doing more with less [online] via shorter bursts of high attention and more efficient encoding to memory." So while we may struggle to focus on any one thing for more than a couple of minutes, we are getting better at focusing intensely for short periods of time. In a world in which we are surrounded by constant distractions, having the ability to quickly pivot our attention from one thing to the next is a valuable asset.

And it's a compelling reason to edit yourself if your conversational style tends to be a little more free-form than direct. The more important your message, the more essential it is that you confine it to a length that makes the best use of the other person's short burst of attention.

My ex-husband used to tell me that I tried to cover all the years of our relationship over the course of one conversation. The power of the current complaint (and it was usually a complaint) was diluted because I kept talking and talking about every related incident that came to mind. I should have kept it short if I had wanted to accomplish something instead of making him feel that every time I said, "We need to talk," I was planning a forty-minute outline of all the mistakes he'd ever made.

At work, I have tried to learn to call employees into my office to talk about one specific thing, or two at the most. During meetings, I have a list of topics to cover and I talk about them in the most concise manner I can, ask if there are questions, and then move on. I've found that since I started that practice, people are consistently on time for meetings and are more engaged. They're also more likely to show up with a positive attitude. Keep your weekly meetings focused and brief and you might never again have to bribe your employees with doughnuts. And most important, I've found my staff is more likely to retain the details of what was discussed.

That's not to say that your conversations should be less than a minute, and they should certainly be longer than eight seconds. But if you prolong a conversation and continue talking for extended periods, you will probably lose the attention of the other person. Their focus will wander while you're still talking. You'll waste their time and your own.

Communication expert Alan Weiss says, "People have a tendency to tell others everything they know," instead of considering what is necessary and what isn't.[3] Take a moment to consider what you need to accomplish in a conversation before you utter your first word. Once you've conveyed your message, resist the temptation to keep talking. In conversation, as in so many things, quality trumps quantity.

I know that not all conversations can be structured and planned and logical. Part of the beauty of real-life conversation compared to e-mail is its spontaneity and unpredictability. There is a lot of space, though, between a robotic conversation that sticks to the facts without embellishment or emotion, and a long, rambling chat in which you start out talking about dog food and somehow find that you've spent ten minutes sharing the details of a novel you read in high school.

We've all had moments when we realized we were blathering. We've all become aware that we're talking about nonsense and seen the light go out of our friend's eyes while we continue to jabber. While the length of a conversation depends on the context and will vary widely, the type of conversation you're having should be determined mutually.

What I mean is: you must be sensitive to the signals you're getting from the other person. Are they indicating that their attention is dwindling and they need to take a break? Are they angling their body away from you, possibly even taking a step away? Are they breaking eye contact frequently? Are they interjecting with "uh-huh" and "yes" to encourage you to reach the end of your sentence? These are signs that the other person's focus has been exhausted.

Remember, a conversation is a game of catch; both parties have to want to play. Keeping it brief demonstrates consideration for your conversation partner. They may be too polite or concerned for your feelings to interrupt you or step away from you. Return their courtesy by not abusing their time and patience.

What if you're the one stuck on the receiving end of a meandering conversation? Perhaps yours are the eyes that have gone dead because, while you know the other person has to stop talking eventually, somehow you just can't *feel* they ever will.

This happens to me on an almost daily basis, but it's not because the people I'm talking to are gabbers. It's because when I finish an interview, I usually have only a couple of minutes between the moment the microphones are turned off and the moment when I have to go back on the air. I need that time to regroup my thoughts so I'll have the energy and attention for the next interview. When a guest wants to keep the dialogue going—no matter how engaging or lively—I say, "I'm so sorry. I would happily continue this conversation over coffee sometime, but I have to go back on the air and I can't talk right now."

I have an easy "out" in the studio, but what about in casual exchanges? For example, I was on a plane recently and the woman next to me began chatting before she even sat down. She had clearly just finished a wonderful visit with her new grandkids and wanted to share her joy with someone else.

Normally, I would happily sit and listen to her loving stories and ooh and aah over her photos. But on that day, I was just too exhausted. Her joy would have only irritated me if I had been forced to listen. So I waited for an opening in the conversation and said, "It sounds like you had a wonderful time. Usually, I would really enjoy hearing about it, but my brain is barely functioning right now. Please forgive me, but I just want to close my eyes and try to get some rest. Is that all right?" Obviously, she agreed and I enjoyed silence for the rest of the trip. As we left the plane, I asked to see a picture of her grandkids and thanked her, sincerely, for allowing me to relax.

Sometimes you can break away politely and respectfully, and sometimes you can't. If you're truly stuck in a seemingly endless conversation and your options are to be openly rude in order to leave or to stay there and take it, try to endure. You might be rewarded for your trouble with new information or an enjoyable few minutes.

Conversations require time and patience; that's part of their value. Some people require more time to articulate their thoughts than others. If you can stay focused and responsive, you will often be richly rewarded. It's worth the wait.

You can also move a stalled conversation forward by asking pointed questions to help your partner get back on track. "What happened when you got home?" you can ask, or "You're killing me with suspense! Skip to the end." Don't wait until you've lost your patience and are liable to say something regrettable. In order to cut an exchange short or move someone along politely, you should be in a relatively positive frame of mind.

If you're truly irritable and can't listen to another word, I'd suggest you simply admit that. Just the other day, when my son was telling me about (another!) new video game he's playing, I said, "I'm cranky and no fun to be around right now. Could you oblige me with silence? I know it's not fair, but I just want to stew in my own cranky juices." His response? "Whatever, Mom."

Brevity is not just the soul of wit, it's a necessary tool for effective communication. As with any rule in this book, there are exceptions. (You might get tired of reading that.) Not every chat should be brief. Many of us know the pleasure of sitting on the couch and talking to a friend for hour after hour. But most of our conversations don't fit that category. In general, it's helpful to know what you want to say before you start, and then keep an eye on the clock as you talk. In the majority of cases, keeping it short will keep it good. And before this becomes ironic, I'll keep this chapter short as well.

10

NO REPEATS

In communications, familiarity breeds apathy.
—WILLIAM BERNBACH

Last year, I called an all-staff meeting to talk with my producers about what was working and what could be improved in the daily operations of our show. One young woman could barely wait for me to open the floor before blurting out: "You criticize us too much! When something goes wrong, you really make me feel horrible."

I was totally taken aback by her response. In my mind, I'm extremely conscious of how much negative feedback I offer. In fact, I keep a notepad by my desk where I track my conversations with employees. My goal is to say at least two positive things to each person every day. How could I have made someone whose work I value feel so bad? I asked her to explain and she reminded me of an incident that had taken place a few weeks prior.

She had arranged for a professor to call in during a

recent show so I could interview him about voter turn-out. But once he was on the line, there was a lot of static. The sound was so bad that it dropped out completely a few times, and it was hard to understand what he was saying.

"What is wrong with his line?" I typed into the on-line chat window that we use to communicate with each other while we're live on the air. "We checked it twice before we went on the air and it sounded good," the producer responded. "But this is terrible," I typed back. "I know," she answered.

After the show was over, I went into the control room to ask more questions. "So, what happened?" I said. The producer answered, "I checked that line multiple times. It was fine." "It sounded awful on the air," I said. "I checked it just a couple of minutes before the show started and it was working," she answered. "Well, there were several moments when I couldn't even understand what he was saying," I said. "I know," she answered.

You'll notice that not once in that entire exchange did I offer explicit criticism. In fact, the producer and I agreed that the interview had not gone well. So why did she come away from our conversation feeling de-moralized? In a word: repetition. I uttered some ver-sion of "that was awful" multiple times. Since she was responsible for the segment, every new iteration felt like a slap. And since we (along with everyone else in the room) agreed on the problem, I was repeating something she already understood, and as a result I was deepening her embarrassment.

After that meeting, I started to take notice of how often I repeated negative feedback. I did it a lot, and it was affecting staff morale. The thing is, it would have never occurred to me that repetition alone could be heard as criticism had this producer not spoken up.

Repetition can be an effective tool in speeches and lectures. Think about how often you've heard a politician repeat the same words or phrases in various forms. These are called talking points and politicians use them because they're as effective as a good advertising slogan: stories about "welfare queens" or "trickle-down economics" or the greed of the so-called 1 percent.

But repetition in this context can also backfire. Remember Marco Rubio's performance during a GOP presidential debate in 2016? Some analysts wryly described it as a "glitch in the matrix" after Rubio repeated the exact same words four times. "Let's dispel this notion that Barack Obama doesn't know what he's doing," Rubio said. "He knows exactly what he's doing."

We can all rib Rubio, but before you start feeling too

smug, consider that most of us unknowingly repeat ourselves daily. Granted, we don't often use the exact same
words, but we repeat the message all the same.

I remember having a conversation with my son after
he got into a fight. A schoolmate was yelling insults at
him on the playground and snatching the ball from him
whenever he could. Finally, my son lost patience and
pushed him. "That was your mistake," I told him. "He
was wrong right up until you put your hands on him.
Then you lost the high ground."

Our conversation continued, as he explained that he
had to go to the principal and write a note of apology
to the other kid. "You just shouldn't have pushed him,"
I said. "If you'd held your temper, he would have been
the one in trouble." And then he said that he would
have to spend a few lunch periods in detention and that
the teacher wanted to talk with me. "That's because
you're the one who decided to make it physical," I said.
Suddenly, he yelled back, "I know! I've heard it a million times now! I'm not stupid!"

I could have lectured him more about losing his temper and raising his voice to me, but I didn't. Because he
was right. I had repeated myself multiple times. (Back
then he was still young enough to get frustrated by repetition. Now he just tunes me out.) I'm willing to bet there

are many kids (and spouses) who don't listen closely because they're "tired of hearing it." In this case, "it" is the same basic message rephrased over and over.

Repetition is the conversational equivalent of marching in place. It's not interesting and it doesn't move anything forward.

We sometimes assume that repeating information helps to drill it into someone's head. After all, we're taught from a young age to repeat the information we want to learn. We make flash cards to learn a foreign language. We repeat important dates in our heads: *The Louisiana Purchase was signed in 1803. The Louisiana Purchase was signed in 1803.* When we have a big test coming up, we cram until the wee hours of the morning, drilling names and dates and equations until our heads swim.

These types of repetition help you to retain new learning for one key reason: you're the one repeating the information. Research shows that when we repeat something multiple times, it ups our chances of remembering it.[1] The benefit increases if we repeat that information to another person, but the benefit isn't shared with the person listening. So, if you're in a meeting and you repeat a deadline to your team four times, you'll probably remember it well but your team members are no more likely to retain it than if you'd mentioned it only once.

There are also limitations to how much repetition benefits memory. In 2014, two neurobiologists at the University of California, Irvine, published a provocative study that gauged the effectiveness of repetition in learning. Study participants were shown pictures of objects such as sunglasses and coffee mugs. They saw each picture no less than three times. Then, researchers showed the participants more pictures and asked them to identify only the exact items that were in the original group. But this time, the researchers inserted "lures," objects that were similar to the original objects but not actually included in the first list, such as an old-fashioned phone instead of a modern one. As it turns out, people had a hard time identifying the lures. They were confident that those comparable objects had been on the original list, even though they hadn't been.[2]

The researchers call this getting the gist instead of remembering fine details. A good example is recognizing a familiar street corner. The study suggests that if you were to visit that corner many times, you might be less able to distinguish it from an intersection that looks similar. That's useful unless you're trying to give your spouse directions. She might ask if there's a drugstore at a particular intersection and your memory may not be accurate.

The effectiveness of repetition can also wane. The first reading of something gives us a great deal of information. But, as psychologists Henry Roediger and Mark McDaniel explain, "When you do the second reading, you read with a sense of 'I know this, I know this.' So basically, you're not processing it deeply, or picking more out of it. Often, the re-reading is cursory—and it's insidious because this gives you the illusion that you know the material very well, when in fact, there are gaps."[3] I'll bet we can all remember listening to someone repeat something to us while, in our heads, we thought, "I know, I know, I know." The first hearing may have been helpful, but the second and third . . . not so much. In fact, research seems to imply that repeating important information will make people more likely to tune out rather than help them remember.

Repetition can make us *feel* like we know the material well. But because our attention wanders after the first reading (or our iteration of it in conversation), our memory of that material becomes less and less precise. It's an important point to consider in the context of conversations, because we frequently repeat ourselves when we're talking to others. And often, when someone hears the same thing for a second and third time, they think, "I already know this," and they stop listening.

It is ironic, in a way, that repetition prompts people to stop listening, because most of us tend to repeat ourselves when we fear we haven't been heard. You tell your coworker to have a report ready by four p.m., but you see no acknowledgment that they heard you. So, you rephrase it: "If it's not ready by four p.m., I won't have time to send it to the corporate office." But again, he or she fails to respond in a way that reassures you. So, you rephrase yet again.

The thing is, just because someone doesn't say, "Yes, I hear and understand what you're saying," it doesn't mean that he or she didn't hear and understand you. People don't always confirm that they've heard important information. The vast majority of the time, there's no need to restate what you've said.

This scenario plays itself out in many settings in our lives. You can find dozens of ways to tell your kid to walk the dogs or tell your spouse to fix a leaky faucet. They may continue to stare at a video screen or football game and not give you the acknowledgment you expect. So you find another way to say it. But perhaps part of the reason they're tuning you out is because they've become accustomed to you telling them the same thing over and over again.

Try to become aware of how often you repeat yourself, and think about what might be prompting you to do it. Do you feel like you're not getting the acknowledgment you need from the other person? Has he or she failed to follow through on things in the past? Are there too many distractions present when you're trying to have a conversation (i.e., saying something important while your kid is playing a video game may not be a good idea)? Are you prone to ramble in your conversations?

Over the next few weeks, get into the habit of pausing for a couple of seconds before you respond to someone. Before you repeat yourself, take a moment to find something new to say. You can even ask your friends to tell you when you're repeating something. I had my son say "echo" every time I started repeating things, and after hearing it a few dozen times, I began to break the habit.

A couple of years ago, I made a New Year's resolution not to repeat the same information more than twice per conversation. I thought it would be easy. My resolution lasted for about two weeks.

It's like when you go on a diet and start keeping a food journal. At first you can't imagine how writing down everything you eat could help because you think you have a pretty good handle on what you consume. But when you tally every cookie, every handful of M&M's, every soda, you realize that you weren't actually aware of what was going into your mouth.

The same is true of repetition. Once I started keeping track of it, I realized I wasn't actually aware of what was coming *out* of my mouth.

Repeating yourself can be a symptom of conversational narcissism. It can be the result of wanting to keep a conversation going but having nothing new to add. This is quite common in the workplace—we've all been in those meetings with someone who doesn't want to stop talking but has nothing else to say. So, they repeat themselves. These meetings are neither enjoyable nor especially productive. Why would you want to reproduce that effect in your personal life?

CRAMMING 101

Many of us can remember pulling all-nighters in which we used flash cards or other repetitive study aids to cram for an upcoming test, all the while sucking down coffee. We may have thought that was a winning strategy, but new research shows that repeatedly drilling names or numbers doesn't help you remember them. If you want to make something stick, spaced repetition is the way to go.

Spaced repetition is a clever variation on cramming

that allows time to pass in between a repeat of information. I know some high-powered executives who swear by it, as well as medical students and even people with mild dementia. There's a popular program called SuperMemo that allows you to use spaced repetition to memorize vocabulary, poetry, and nearly any other information you input.[4]

Here's how I use it. I'm terrible at remembering names. So, when I learn someone's name for the first time, I repeat it immediately. Then I let some time pass, a minute or so, and I say it again. If I'm able to use their name in conversation four or five times, while allowing a little time to pass in between each iteration, I have a much better chance at really learning their name. (But not a great chance, because I have a mental block when it comes to people's names. That's just a warning, in case we ever meet.)

The same principle can also be applied to the workplace. Let's say there are three important points you need to convey to your coworkers. You state them at the start of the meeting ("Here's what we're going to cover"), then you explain each point, and at the end, you repeat them one more time ("To recap, here's the important information"). Your colleagues are more likely to remember what you've said if you give structure and space to your repetition.

Repetition is often boring, unnecessary, and counterproductive. It seems to be most effective as a memory aid for the speaker and not the listener, and that's why it's often a conversation killer. The only way to make sure you're not teaching people to tune you out is to pay attention to what you're saying. Listen to yourself first. You may be surprised by what you hear and hear and hear.

11

THAT'S A GREAT QUESTION

No one is dumb who is curious. The people who don't
ask questions remain clueless throughout their lives.
—NEIL DEGRASSE TYSON

There's an old trick that reporters use to get people to
say interesting things. We start our questions with one
of six words: who, what, where, when, why, and how.

This practice is known as asking open-ended questions, and you've probably heard of it or used some form
of it yourself, whether in a job interview or on a date.
The genius of open-ended questions is that they can't be
answered with a simple yes or no. The most uncompli-
cated questions often elicit a complicated response, just
as a detailed question can result in a one-word answer.

For example, if I'm interviewing someone about a
tornado that came through their town, I could ask, "The
winds were moving at more than one hundred miles per
hour. It looks like your house was just torn apart. Were
you scared?" Most likely, I'll get this answer: "Yeah, I
was really scared. It was scary."

But if I ask this person, "What was it like to be so close to the eye of a tornado?" chances are good that I'll get a more interesting response. I could also ask, "What did you hear?" or "How did it feel?" These are all open-ended questions because they open up the discussion. They provide the individual the needed space to describe what happened in his or her own words. Maybe "scary" isn't the right word to describe their feelings. Open-ended questions encourage people to tell their own stories.

I make a conscious effort to use this tactic on a daily basis, outside of the radio studio. Ever had trouble getting your kid to talk about what happened in school? Me, too. I've learned to use open-ended questions like "What happened in history class?" or "What did the teacher say?" Granted, sometimes he answers with "nothing." But often, my simple, direct question will draw out a multiword answer.

Closed-ended questions—often yes-or-no questions—are also important tools and can be used effectively in many different circumstances. "Is your phone broken?" "Do you need a ride home?" Those are just two examples out of probably trillions that are best answered with a yes or no. As with everything else in conversation, context matters and no advice is absolute. If you're just trying to get information as quickly and efficiently as possible, a closed-ended question is the perfect choice. It's specific, to the point, and yields quick results.

But there's another aspect of closed-ended questions that you may not have considered: they typically allow you to retain control of the conversation. Open-ended questions transfer control to the person responding (in our "game of catch" analogy, asking an open-ended question is the equivalent of throwing the ball to your partner). The floor is open for the other person to take as much or as little time as they like to answer a question that starts with "why" or "how."

When I moved to Atlanta to start a radio show at Georgia Public Broadcasting, there was a relatively small group of people who were upset that our news shows would replace a student-run music station. One guy in particular sent me angry messages on a daily basis, sometimes tweeting out negative comments about me and the station.

I asked him to have lunch with me, and I have to admit that I was a little nervous about meeting with him. He was clearly angry and some of that anger was directed at me, personally. I feared an argument and wanted to avoid it at all costs. So, I restricted myself almost entirely to simple, open-ended questions: "Why are you angry?" "What do you know about the new plans for the station?" "What will change for you now that news will be broadcast during the day?" "What can I tell you about the show that I'm creating for the station?"

I learned all kinds of interesting things about him, like the fact that he makes a hobby of collecting and repairing old radios. I also walked away with a greater understanding of why he was so upset about the change to the station and why he loved the music programming so much. Asking questions took the pressure off of me, since I didn't have to offer a lot of information. And I made sure to let him speak for himself by using questions that didn't attempt to characterize his feelings or thoughts. We ended up having a lovely lunch together.

I don't mean to suggest that using open-ended questions is always the best strategy, or that all open-ended questions are good questions. Most of us have heard some terrible questions during job interviews that weren't improved by the fact that they were open-ended. "What's your biggest weakness?" "Where do you see yourself in five years?" "Why do you want this job?" Those questions are open-ended, but very few applicants will answer them honestly. (For the record, "How does/did that make you feel?" is also a terrible question. It may be open-ended, but it's become so cliché that it's been vacated of any meaning.)

Of course, in order to improve your questions, you have to ask questions in the first place. I've found that most people tend not to ask a lot of questions. There's no telling why, although I would guess it has something to do with our tendency toward a narcissistic conversational style. Whatever the cause, it's a terrible shame, because questions are powerful.

Questions allow you to express concern and show your interest and care. I use them to draw out introverts, encourage children, and give attention to the overlooked. When a friend is in need, I sometimes limit myself almost entirely to questions. Surely one of the most compassionate and patient conversationalists in recent history, Fred Rogers (of *Mister Rogers' Neighborhood*) once described the power of questions in this way: "In times of stress, the best thing we can do for each other is to listen with our ears and our hearts and to be assured that our questions are just as important as our answers."

Sincere questions can even open up conversation with those people who don't like us very much. Social psychologist Robert Cialdini wrote a book called *Influence: The Psychology of Persuasion*. He has two suggestions for winning over a person who dislikes you: give honest compliments and *ask for advice*. Ask questions! Ask what book they'd recommend, ask how they would handle a particular situation at work. Ask if they have a favorite vacation spot or ask what kind of gift you should buy for a twelve-year-old nephew.[1]

I bet there are all kinds of things you'd like to know and you're in luck because you're surrounded by people who know things. If you don't ask questions, you might not get the full benefit of the expertise in your circle of friends and coworkers.

There is an art to asking questions. I pride myself on doing enough research to be able to ask questions of even celebrities that they've never been asked before. One of my favorite compliments is when someone looks at me in surprise and says, "Wow! Great question. I'm not sure how to answer that." Asking a good question requires careful listening and honest curiosity.

If you've asked a good question, be sure you allow the other person enough time to answer. Don't be afraid of silence. Often, silence means the other person is thinking and, by definition, their answer will be thoughtful. "There have been studies that show that if you're presenting a listener with a series of words or tones, and you take an extended silence, certain populations of cells in their brains start looking for the signal," says neuroscientist Seth Horowitz, "and if it doesn't happen in a certain period of time, it triggers arousal centers, emotional centers. Silence is an important part of communication, and something people don't pay attention to."[2] He's saying that silence wakes up parts of our brains that may have been sleeping. If you allow space for silence in your conversations, you may engage more of your own mind and that of the other person's.

Using open-ended questions is a discipline that takes practice. Not every question can begin with "who," "what," "where," "why," "when," and "how." I strive to begin about half of my questions that way, and even that is sometimes a struggle. But the quality of the response you receive after a good, open-ended question is immediately noticeable.

"We get wise by asking questions," wrote novelist James Stephens, "and even if [they] are not answered, we get wise, for a well-packed question carries its answer on its back as a snail carries its shell."[3] Sometimes a question can be an inspiration, an impetus to further exploration and discovery. Some of the greatest innovations of humankind began with simple questions.

12

YOU CAN'T KNOW EVERYTHING

I was gratified to be able to answer promptly. I said I don't know.

—MARK TWAIN

In 2009, the once wildly popular Domino's Pizza chain was struggling to survive. Sales were down and stock prices had hit an all-time low. The pizza itself had tied for last place in a national taste test.

Something radical had to be done, and fast. And so, in an unorthodox move, the company launched an ad campaign that bluntly admitted its mistake: it was making bad pizza.

In a television commercial, they quoted customers who compared the pies to "cardboard" and called them the "worst excuse for pizza" they'd ever had and said they were "totally void of flavor." The ad showed images of harsh criticisms from customers printed out, framed, and hung on office walls. The voice-over announced that Domino's was debuting a new recipe and asked customers to give them a second chance.

The chief executive officer of Domino's later said he was scared to death to run that ad. It could have backfired horribly. But it didn't. That campaign has been credited with fueling one of the most incredible turnarounds in restaurant history. The following year, sales rose almost 14 percent and their stock price jumped by 130 percent. The company gambled on honesty and it paid off. As John Glass of Morgan Stanley observed, "People are so used to not being told the truth in advertising. The candor worked."[1]

If you're a parent, then you've probably explained to your kids that telling lies creates more problems than it solves. The same principle holds true when it comes to grown-up conversations. That's not to say that you need to tell your husband exactly what you think of his singing voice, but, in most cases, telling the truth is the right call.

I understand, of course, that it's not possible to tell the whole truth at all times. But telling the occasional fib about why your business lunch ran late or why you didn't make it to your kid's soccer game is very different from telling someone a "fact" that you either know isn't true or that you don't know to be true. I think it is perfectly possible to avoid saying things that you don't know for sure and get comfortable with saying "I don't know."

There are two important reasons to do this: first, you establish a foundation of trust and honesty, and second, you admit your own fallibility. It could be that the Domino's ad campaign resonated because people responded to the company's humility in addition to their forthrightness. Owning up to a mistake or a lack of knowledge might feel like admitting weakness, but it can create a powerful empathetic bond.

When I interview someone on live radio, they are typically very careful with their words. There's a big, intimidating microphone in front of them, producers staring at them through glass, and they have a pressing awareness that lots of people are listening. All of these factors serve as reminders that anything they say will soon become part of the public record, archived on the Internet for years. So, they're usually pretty cautious about what they choose to share.

Many of us are not that careful in casual conversation. A friend mentions car trouble and we immediately offer our thoughts on carburetors and alternators as if we're mechanics. A coworker refers to some news about immigration policy and we start spouting opinions and facts as though we work for the Immigration

and Naturalization Service. You don't remember a sta-
tistic exactly? That's okay, just estimate! Did you only
skim through a blog about plane travel? No problem!
You've traveled on planes many times. You know how
it should work.

While it is always tempting to add your two cents in
a conversation, I strongly advise you not to say things
that you don't know to be factually correct; nor should
you offer opinions on subjects about which you know
very little. To be perfectly clear, reading the first couple of paragraphs of an article that someone posted on
Facebook is not the same as "knowing" something to
be true. And limited experience does not make you an
expert. Just because you've had a baby doesn't mean
that you know everything about pregnancy; golfing
a few times a year doesn't make you a pro. When you
pretend to know more than you do, you will eventually
give someone bad advice or prevent them from seeking
the guidance of a real, bona fide expert. In the words
of the great poet Alexander Pope, "A little learning is a
dangerous thing."

There are any number of reasons why we pretend
to know things we don't or act as if we possess greater
knowledge of a subject than we really do. The first is
simple: we want to impress people. It's natural to want
other people to think we're smart. The irony is that when

you say things that aren't entirely accurate, you appear less intelligent than if you'd said nothing at all. It's like when a young kid uses big words but pronounces them incorrectly.

Another reason we tend to posture is because we are reluctant to ask for help. In his book *Help: The Original Human Dilemma*, Garret Keizer argues that most people actively avoid seeking assistance from others. "There is a tendency to act as if [asking for help] is a deficiency," Keizer told the *New York Times* in an interview. "That is exacerbated if a business environment is highly competitive within as well as without. There is an understandable fear that if you let your guard down, you'll get hurt, or that this information you don't know . . . will be used against you."[2]

Asking for help in a professional setting might betray what you don't know about your job, which could put you at risk. But many of us refuse to ask for help in even mundane situations. (Raise your hand if you refuse to ask for directions when you're lost.) Admitting that you don't know something and asking someone else for information can feel awkward. It can feel like exposing a weakness. But not admitting it, or worse, saying something that may not be true, is a near-certain way to erode the respect of your peers.

Sometimes we offer up our uninformed thoughts

because we genuinely want to help whoever prevails upon *us* for help. Let's say your friend from out of town asks you for a restaurant recommendation. Your instinctive response is to name a place that you pass on the way home from work every day. You've never eaten there, but it looks like a good place. The prudent thing to do, of course, is to admit that you've never eaten there, but you've checked out the menu and noticed the parking lot is always crowded. Yet often, we gloss over those details. What if your friend, trusting your recommendation, ate at this restaurant, only to discover that the food is atrocious? How would that affect her opinion of you? At the very least, she'll think you have terrible taste.

Now, imagine this: Mike says to Mandy, "I want to see this movie, but I'm not sure I should spend the money. Do you know if it's any good?" Mandy has not seen the movie. She saw a thirty-second trailer and she read a comment on Facebook from a friend who didn't like it. So, she has a choice to make. Does she admit that she doesn't know if it's good, or does she pretend she's seen it and say, "That movie is terrible, don't bother"?

I'm not pulling that example out of my imagination. It happened to me recently. How do I know the other person hadn't seen the movie? Because after she told me that it was awful, I said, "So, you've seen it? Why was it so bad?" At that point, she admitted she hadn't seen it. And I'll admit that my opinion of that person sank a little. Even though she hadn't technically lied, it *felt* like she had.

In Steven Levitt and Stephen Dubner's book *Think Like a Freak*, there's a chapter called "The Three Hardest Words in the English Language." You might think those words are "I love you," but the authors argue that those words are actually "I don't know." They cite research in which children between the ages of five and eight were asked a series of questions and up to 75 percent of them answered yes or no even when they couldn't possibly have known the answer.

The woman behind that research is Amanda Waterman, who teaches developmental psychology at the University of Leeds. And lest you think that only children would be so silly as to pretend they know stuff that they clearly don't, Waterman conducted a series of tests with adults as well. When she tested the grown-ups, one out of four pretended they knew what they could not possibly know. You might think the fear of being exposed would prevent us from lying, but for 25 percent of us, that fear isn't strong enough.

Waterman says we are less likely to admit that we don't know something when we're talking to an individual with more power or higher rank than us. "Perhaps

[we] feel slightly disadvantaged," she says. "[People] feel like they want to show what they can do. They don't feel as comfortable admitting when they don't know something."

Steven Levitt suggests that the temptation to pretend to be an expert is especially strong in the business world. He says the MBA (master of business administration) students he teaches are very good "at faking like they know the answer when they have no idea." But he goes on to say that the "fake it till you make it" mentality is completely counterproductive. "It might keep your job for another week or another month," he says, "but that's not the point. The goal is to be good and to improve and to learn and to make things better and the only way to do that is to start by saying, 'I don't know.'"[3]

I would take this conclusion one step further. When you pretend that you know something you don't, you not only limit your potential, you also risk taking advantage of someone's trust in you.

Let's return to the conversation I had about the new movie for a moment. If I hadn't asked my friend more questions about how she'd formed her opinion, I probably wouldn't have gone to see the film. I would have trusted her erroneous advice. And that would have been too bad because I did see it and I really enjoyed it. In fact, I loved it so much, I went to see it a second time a couple of weeks later.

What about when the stakes are higher than a movie recommendation? Many doctors admit they have difficulty saying they don't know what's wrong with a patient. In an interview in the *Huffington Post*, neurologist Nicholas Capozzoli suggested that this issue is common among his peers. "Doctors tend to be uncomfortable admitting uncertainty to themselves or to their patients. Too often, they feel it's a threat to their skill, authority, or expert status to say they simply don't know what's causing the symptoms or that there is no magic bullet to cure them."[4]

Dr. Stuart Foxman wrote about this in a column for the College of Physicians and Surgeons of Ontario. He described a physician who experimented with saying "I don't know" when he truly wasn't sure of an answer. The result? Several of his patients said they trusted him more. "Patients are aware that every doctor has limitations in their knowledge base," Foxman writes, "but they want to feel like you're doing your best for them. That comes when you say 'I don't know—but I'll find out.'"[5]

Conversations are the basis of relationships, and relationships are built on trust. You will find that the more open you are about the limitations of your knowledge, the more weight people will give to your opinion when you offer it. If you don't know something, just say "I don't know." Those three words can strengthen the bond between you and another person. And just as important, they are a gateway to further exploration and growth. You can't learn unless you admit that you have something to learn.

13

STAY OUT OF THE WEEDS

The ability to simplify means to eliminate the unnecessary so that the necessary may speak.

—HANS HOFMANN

Have you ever heard of a shaggy dog story? That's what you call a story that includes all kinds of extraneous, unnecessary details and irrelevant tangents that lead up to an anticlimactic ending. There are many examples of this kind of tale that actually include a shaggy dog, but the most classic example, in my opinion, comes from Mark Twain.

In his now-classic 1872 book, *Roughing It*, Twain writes about his travels through the western United States. In one town, Twain met a number of people who knew a man named Jim Blaine; they said he had a story that was not to be missed. And so Twain waited impatiently for an opportunity to hear the tale in person. Finally, Twain caught Blaine at just the right time and sat down to listen to the "stirring story of his grandfather's old ram." If you've read the book, then you know that what follows is an unbroken block of text nearly fifteen hundred words long. Here's a sample:

Grandfather fetched [the ram] from Illinois—got him of a man by the name of Yates—Bill Yates— maybe you might have heard of him; his father was a deacon—Baptist—and he was a rustler, too; a man had to get up ruther early to get the start of old Thankful Yates; it was him that put the Greens up to jining teams with my grandfather when he moved west. Seth Green was prob'ly the pick of the flock; he married a Wilkerson—Sarah Wilkerson—good cretur, she was—one of the likeliest heifers that was ever raised in old Stoddard, everybody said that knowed her.

Blaine never finishes, because he falls asleep midstory. (Turns out, that's what happens every time the tale is told, and Twain is understandably irritated about the prank that's been played on him.) Blaine's story is an extreme example of something most of us do on a regular basis: offer too much detail and cite too many unnecessary facts. Just as with Blaine, too much detail can ruin a good story and bore your audience.

Journalists refer to this tendency as "getting into the

weeds"—relaying a story in so much detail that it becomes uninteresting or impossible to follow. When you get into the weeds, you've lost the story, or main path, and you're wandering aimlessly in a field of trivial detail. It's hard enough to keep people's attention when you're talking about something relevant and important. Imagine how much harder it becomes when you start rattling off names and dates that aren't pertinent.

My job requires me to be very aware of how I communicate. But it wasn't until I set out on a journey to improve my conversation skills that I noticed how often I weave unnecessary details into my conversations. Specifically, I realized, I bog down stories with a lot of unneeded, somewhat irritating facts.

Perhaps you can relate. Getting into the weeds often sounds something like this: "We went to Italy in 2006. No, was it 2007? Wait, it must have been 2005 because it was just after I took that job in Boston. I think that's right. Sharon would know for sure." By the time you get back to the real story, your friend is staring at you with glassy eyes and considering making a break for it to get a latte.

The business psychiatrist Mark Goulston says we only have about forty seconds to speak during a conversation before we run the risk of dominating the exchange.

He describes the first twenty seconds as the green light, when the other person likes you and is enjoying what you have to say. The next twenty seconds are the yellow light, when "the other person is beginning to lose interest or think you're long-winded." At forty seconds, Goulston says, the light turns red and it's time to stop talking.[1]

Take a moment to gauge just how long forty seconds is. Look at the second hand on your clock or watch, start to tell a story, and stop when you've hit forty seconds. That's not a lot of time! If you waste it with superfluous detail, you'll never get to the meat of your message.

There are any number of reasons why people babble. I've mentioned one of the most likely already: it's inherently pleasurable to talk about ourselves and most people enjoy talking. But some talk excessively when they're nervous; anxiety keeps the words flowing out of their mouths. Others do it because they want to impress people with the breadth and depth of their knowledge on a subject. And some people have simply never learned how to listen and are uncomfortable with silence.

Whatever the reason, extraneous detail can be the death of a good conversation, just as all of Jim Blaine's tangents killed what might have been a great story . . . if he'd ever finished it.

Of course, there are instances in which it's important

to sweat the details. We all hope our politicians go into the weeds before they vote on legislation, for example. A lawyer arguing a court case should study and articulate the minutiae of the law, and we certainly hope that our doctors and accountants concern themselves with even the smallest technicalities. But most of us don't want to hear a congressman talk about changes to the Aldrich-Vreeland Act or listen patiently while our doctor debates which scalpel he'll use for our surgery. We want him or her to discuss these things with peers, but we don't want to hear about them. Our daily conversations can quickly get buried underneath too much detail and suffocate us for lack of air.

For some, "the weeds" are actually a comfortable place to hold a conversation. I'm sure you have at least one friend or family member who takes great pleasure in naming each task he or she accomplished that day or in reciting a list of things he or she has yet to do. You say, "How's it going?" And this person answers, "I've been so busy today! I got up early and made breakfast. I have to make a special meal for my dog because he's got some digestive trouble and needs a powder mixed in. Then I had to take my laptop in for repairs. About a week ago, it started freezing whenever I opened my CD player. Then, I went . . ." I won't torture you with the rest of that example. It's difficult to read it without getting bored, isn't it?

For the most part, no one cares about those things except you. Would you buy a book that comprised two hundred pages of someone else's to-do list? Probably not. I don't want to hear about cleaning your cat box, going to the ATM, or picking up some lettuce from the grocery store. Those details aren't even interesting to the cat.

That's not to say that it's not rewarding *for you* to take note of what you've done or need to do. Many productivity experts recommend making a habit out of writing down what you do every day. This gives you a sense of achievement and clears the mental to-do list from your head so you can focus on other things. But instead of writing our accomplishments on a tablet, we sometimes download our data onto other people.

Detailing your daily tasks out loud might feel good, but it's rarely the stuff of good conversation. What can someone say when they've heard your to-do list? "Wow, that's a lot of stuff"? It might even seem as though you're expecting praise for having accomplished so much or sympathy for all you have left to do. And you have almost certainly exceeded Mark Goulston's forty-second time limit.

I want to be very careful not to imply that sharing the details of something about which you care deeply is never okay. Sometimes it's helpful to be able to tell someone all the things we've done or need to do, and it's often a gesture of love on their part to listen to us and show support. I can't tell you how many times I've listened with half an ear while my son described the ins and outs of a complicated table game. While I think it's important to listen to him, and I will continue to do so no matter how many times he tells me about each character's attack power, I do so because I'm his mother and I love him more than anyone else on the planet, not because I have any illusions that our exchange constitutes a good conversation.

Listening to details is also a service you can perform for a friend in need. A loved one who has been diagnosed with cancer might need to talk about every last aspect of her treatment and prognosis. She might need to talk about all of her concerns, even the mundane ones. Someone who's lost a loved one may tell you all kinds of particulars about that person's life and work. In that case, listening is an act of love.

However, you don't have to sit patiently while your friend tells you about all she had to go through to get her vehicle registration. She might want to complain about how long she sat on hold and how she had to listen to the same soft-rock song six times, but you don't have to listen. You *can*, but you can also tell her to skip to the end of the story.

Reciting our errands is just one way in which we venture into the weeds. Another common mistake is to relate everything we know about a subject in one big conversational dump. I've seen this a lot in the radio studio, especially when a guest is nervous. I'll bring up a topic and then my guest will proceed to tell me everything he or she knows about it. My job is to cut this person off before we both lose sight of the path.

The same thing happens frequently in our personal conversations. Someone asks if we have a pet and we tell them the names of our pets, their ages, their breeds, and their personalities. We talk about the amount of RAM (random-access memory) and shadow RAM we have when we're asked if we have a desktop or a laptop.

Most of us do it, and it's not usually because we're trying to bore people. I doubt anyone goes into a conversation and thinks, "Boy! I'm really going to bore this guy to death. He'll wish he never saw me today." But make no mistake: those details are probably boring to everyone but you. If the point of a conversation is to engage someone else so you can have an effective and enlightening exchange, the trivialities can quickly become counterproductive.

The damage is worse if you actually have important information to share. If you want to give someone flight details, stick to the name of the airline, the time the flight leaves, and the flight number. If you throw in the amount the ticket cost, the length of the layover, the best place to park, and the flight number for the return trip, the essential information could get lost.

Think of it this way: Imagine you wanted someone to remember a number. Would you recite a hundred different numbers or just the one that mattered? If you threw a hundred Ping-Pong balls at someone, would it make it easier or harder for someone to catch one in particular?

It's not just to-do lists and boring details that lead us into the weeds. We can also end up there when we feel compelled to correct the fine print of someone else's story. Imagine a friend is telling you about a scary skiing accident. He says that after he was airlifted to the nearest hospital, he received an emergency MRI to see if his ribs were broken. You jump in and say, "Well, actually, the MRI wouldn't show your ribs. An MRI only shows soft tissues. Are you sure it wasn't an X-ray?" You have just steered a conversation (and possibly a friendship) into the weeds.

The same principle holds true for more routine exchanges. It can be tempting to correct someone's grammar or misuse of a technical term or mispronunciation. But I beg you to resist the temptation.

Let me go a step further and suggest that you eliminate the phrase "Well, actually . . ." from your lexicon. I don't usually give advice about specific words or phrases to use or avoid, but I'll make an exception here. Much like "I'm not a racist, but . . . ," nothing good will come after the words "well, actually." If you really need to correct someone because something bad will happen if they don't have the accurate information, find another way or wait until they've finished their story. If it's trivial, a correction is not necessary. No one needs to interrupt a story about dinner in order to explain that real champagne only comes from France.

The onus is on you to determine what information is essential and what is unnecessary. That can be difficult sometimes. But if you're thinking about it, you're already making progress. All too often, we continue to spout information without consciously considering if we should.

The next time you find yourself providing a lot of detail about a personal matter, take a close look at the other person's face. Are they looking at something else besides you? Are they stifling a yawn?

If so, they may be trying to escape. Forget about what year you bought your first Toyota and move the story along. Your friends, family, coworkers, baristas, and cashiers will thank you.

14

TRAVEL TOGETHER

> Clearing your head of distractions in order to notice and understand the people you are with can feel inefficient—there are so many other people and issues to think about. But being present makes you effective.
>
> —MARGARET HEFFERNAN

I find that folksy terminology often describes human behavior more aptly than any diagnostic manual ever could. I began the last chapter with the phrase "shaggy dog story." This one starts with a similarly tactile term: "woolgathering."

When used to describe behavior in a conversation, woolgathering refers to the habit of indulging in random thoughts or daydreaming. When you're woolgathering, you may be looking directly at the person who's speaking and even nodding your head from time to time, but you don't actually hear a word that person is saying. You're caught up in your thoughts, in your own world. You are gathering wool.

The term comes from the practice of wandering from bush to bush in a pasture, gathering the tufts of wool left behind by passing sheep. There is no direction or defined pathway; you just amble over to any old bush where you see a clump of white and then move on to the next.

The difference between going into the weeds and woolgathering in a conversation is that in the first scenario, the speaker becomes distracted; in the latter, it's the listener who struggles to focus.

When I refer to woolgathering, I'm not talking about a momentary interruption or loss of focus; I'm talking about the kinds of distracting thoughts that carry you deeper into your own head and farther away from the conversation. Another common phrase for woolgathering is "going down the rabbit hole." Like Alice daydreaming her way into Wonderland, you fall down, down, down, away from the conversation that's happening in real time.

This is an area where I have particular trouble. I'm the type of person some might call "scatterbrained." I have adult attention deficit disorder (AADD), and at times it can be very difficult for me to focus. My head becomes easily tangled with the threads of a million divergent thoughts racing off in all directions. If I'm not careful, I can follow one of these threads and, within seconds, find myself miles away from a conversation. You'll be telling me about getting your car repaired and I'll respond with a comment about Michael Jackson's performance in *The Wiz*. (Yes, this actually happened.)

In my early work as a reporter, this wasn't such a big deal. I was never live on the air for very long—all of my interviews were recorded and edited. However, when I became the host of a live talk show, my tendency toward distraction became a very big deal indeed.

I will never forget one particular interview with a foreign correspondent about the war in Afghanistan. I'm not sure when I first lost my train of thought, but at some point he stopped talking, waiting for my response—and I realized I had no idea what he'd just said. I asked a question that I thought would take us in a new direction, only to discover that he'd already answered it. I know that because he prefaced his response with, "Well, as I just explained . . ."

Tens of thousands of people were listening. I was mortified.

Perhaps this sounds familiar. While there are substantially fewer witnesses to most people's woolgathering moments, I have yet to meet someone who, at some point, hasn't been called out for spacing out.

How do you know if, like me, you're especially prone to woolgathering? There are actually a few tests designed to measure your ability to ignore irrelevant information. One is called the Stroop Color and Word Test (if you Google it, you'll find that there are many different versions of the test available online). In the exercise, you're asked to identify a word by the color of the letters, not the word itself. For example, the word "white" might be printed in orange letters. Your task is to identify the color orange, even though the voice inside your head—the one that distracts us in conversations—will be focused on the word "white." The faster you try to answer each question, the more likely you are to rely on that voice and make a mistake.

People who take the Stroop test find it to be tougher than they'd expected. You could read the scientific studies and pore over the conclusions, but I can boil down the results for you in one simple sentence: most humans are distractible to some degree.

But have you ever known someone who had an uncanny ability to filter out distractions? I had a friend in college who could have written her dissertation while seated in the middle of Times Square. She, and people like her, have a high degree of a quality known as "latent inhibition." Your latent inhibition determines your ability to filter out noises and other interruptions. If your latent inhibition is high, you probably have no trouble working in an open-floor-plan office. If it's low, you might need headphones to block out distractions and concentrate on your work. For those with extremely low latent inhibition, a distraction as minor as a pigeon on the ledge outside your boss's office might prevent you from focusing on what he or she is saying.

Harvard psychologist Shelley Carson has demonstrated that creative, highly intelligent people are seven times more likely to have low latent inhibition.[1] Translation: the smarter and more creative you are, the more trouble you may have in tuning out distractions. In some ways, the stereotype of the "airhead" creative is true—those of us with strong creative impulse are more likely to get lost in the endless hallways of our own minds.

It's natural and quite common to be easily distracted, and it doesn't reflect negatively on your character. It might even say something positive about you, if you're the glass-half-full type. But it certainly doesn't help if you're trying to have a good conversation.

A good conversation requires focus, and it demands that two people focus on the same subject at the same time. Both people have to be willing and prepared to ignore a good portion of what passes through their heads. Why? Because distraction is inherently individual. Your random thoughts and connections will almost never match what's going on in another person's head. That doesn't mean a random thought can't become a great addition to a conversation, but that's not what usually happens.

When someone mentions a specific object or place—a minor detail in their story—you may find yourself scurrying down a rabbit hole. Your friend says she saw her ex at a local coffee shop and that reminds you of the time you saw a celebrity in that coffee shop. You become focused on the effort to insert your story while your friend is describing a tough and awkward experience. She says, "I guess I can't go to that place again," and you respond, "But you might see someone famous, like I did!" You've allowed the random thought to derail the conversation and you might have caused your friend to question your investment in your relationship.

I want to make it clear that, in the right context, a tangent can be a wonderful thing. Something your friend says to you fires up the neurons in your brain and gives you a flash of insight. When you share it, your friend also feels inspired. This kind of conversational improvisation can be an electric, galvanizing experience. But it is one that generally occurs when your flash of insight is related in a substantial way to what your friend was saying. You're not completely changing trains, just wandering together to an unexpected track. It is a shared adventure.

Learning to hone your focus offers benefits that extend far beyond better conversations. A study conducted in 2007 reported that exercising good self-control can lead to better relationships, increased mental health, decreased stress, and better grades, if you're in school.[2] And that's not all: knowing how to tap your willpower can make you less likely to abuse drugs and alcohol, suffer from eating disorders, or break the law. For the purposes of that study, self-control was defined as "the ability to control or override one's thoughts, emotions, urges, and behavior." That's exactly what you're doing when you choose not to follow the thoughts in your head when someone is talking to you.

Incidentally, that same study revealed just how difficult this discipline can be. Your thoughts can literally wear you out. In fact, our brains consume 20 percent of our calories. Researchers found that exerting self-control actually reduces glucose levels in the body. Glucose is a simple sugar that serves as an energy source. Tuning out distractions and narrowing your focus *consumes energy*. In one famous experiment, participants were tempted with freshly baked chocolate cookies and then asked to resist the sweet treats and eat radishes instead. All participants were then given a puzzle. Those who had resisted the cookies struggled with the test; they were too tired to try.

No wonder we have a hard time concentrating on a conversation at the end of a long day—we don't have the energy left to summon our attention.

A good conversation is a smoothly flowing river. It can even be a rough river, with white water and sharp turns. But it shouldn't be diverted or dammed up. And you should never jump to another boat and expect your friend to jump after you. You are in it together, through all the twists and turns.

In order to keep the conversation going, you must learn to let thoughts pass through your mind without distracting you. It's not easy, but it *is* possible to train yourself to ignore disruptive thoughts. I can say this based on my own experience because, as someone with AADD, I have had to work hard on this.

Part of what makes it so difficult to resist the temptation to allow our thoughts to carry us away, or woolgather, is the rapid-fire nature of conversations. In the United States and around the world, conversations take place at lightning speed. When researchers recorded conversations in ten different languages in places like Italy, Denmark, Japan, Korea, Papua New Guinea, Namibia, and the United States, they discovered that the average gap between one person ending a sentence and the other responding is about 200 milliseconds.[3]

The country with the shortest gap is Japan, with 7 milliseconds, which means they're basically talking on top of each other. And even in the nation with the longest gap, Denmark, it was only 470 milliseconds. That's less than half a second! Just for context, it takes 600 milliseconds to dredge up a single word from our memory banks. So, if we respond in only 200 milliseconds, then we are quite literally not taking the time to think before we speak.

How can we possibly respond that quickly? Stephen C. Levinson of the Max Planck Institute for Psycholinguistics says that "we build our responses *during* our partner's turn." Levinson suggests that "we listen to [someone else's] words while simultaneously crafting our own, so that when our opportunity comes, we seize it as quickly as it's physically possible to." That makes sense to me, but I do disagree with Stephen on one point. I don't believe we can listen to someone while we're crafting our response. If we're always thinking about what we're going to say next, I believe we're only ever half-listening in an exchange.

Humans have always been prone to distraction, but technology has exacerbated that. In some ways, we now expect our real-life conversations to match the experience we have online. Research shows that most of us scroll through about half of the articles we "read" on the Internet.[4] And guess what's the most popular feature on the Web? Clicking on links.[5] Think about that for a moment: our favorite thing to do when we're reading about something is to click on a link that takes us to a tangential page. And before we finish reading that, we'll click another link that takes us somewhere else. The Internet encourages our brains to follow tangents, but that doesn't work very well in conversation.

It's totally natural to have dozens of thoughts crowding your brain while you're listening to someone else talk. It's natural to become distracted when a butterfly flutters by or a guy in a funny T-shirt walks past. It's also natural to think of something that you'd much rather talk about, or get really excited about something that occurred to you while you were listening. None of these types of distraction are inherently bad or even counterproductive. But attempting to incorporate those random thoughts into a conversation won't make the conversation better. It's difficult for someone else to follow the meanderings of your mind, so if you indulge in woolgathering, you will likely wander off and leave them behind.

For some, allowing the conversation to flow freely is difficult because it requires them to give up control. In conversations, we often like to be the driver of the car; woolgathering can be a method of keeping hold of the wheel. If we feel like taking a turn, we do it. We can take an exit at any time by changing the subject. This can be especially tempting if a thought arises that we think is particularly clever or interesting. It's hard to resist making that joke or inserting a witty comment, even if it will disrupt the flow of the conversation. Often, we don't realize we're interrupting! We're just interjecting an astute comment that enriches and enlivens the conversation, right? It's a subtle form of conversational narcissism.

The line between a diversion and a legitimate response can be blurry at times. It's not always clear where a conversation is heading, so it's impossible to know if your remark will change its course. That line becomes easier to detect if you are really listening.

Here's a good, general rule of thumb: In a healthy conversation, you're present. You are listening to what's being said at that moment. If you're letting a thought distract you or if you're focused on what you want to say next, you're not listening.

It is possible to train your mind to be less easily distracted. Meditation is one very effective method. It teaches you to observe your thoughts and release them rather than hold on to them. But if you're not one for meditation, you can simply start to take notice of what's happening inside your head. Don't try to change anything, just be aware. The sooner you notice a distraction, the better chance you have of allowing it to pass from your mind before it carries your brain and body with it.

Using MRI technology, scientists have not only identified the part of the brain that helps us stay focused (the ventrolateral prefrontal cortex), they've also found that mental activity has its own kind of momentum.[6] For example, once you think about getting a glass of water, your body starts preparing to move and your mouth might even water in anticipation. The farther you get down a mental pathway, the harder it is to stop the momentum. If you make a practice of paying attention to your thoughts, you'll notice when a distraction slips in before your physiological response is in full swing. That's what it means to be "mindful."

Once you're aware of the thoughts that come into

your head, don't fight them or try to "clear your mind." You can't stop your brain from thinking, and actively resisting your thoughts can be very distracting. Instead, when a thought comes into your head, simply say to yourself, "That's a thought," and then try to return your focus to the conversation.

Also—at this point, I hope it goes without saying— the best conversations are unplugged. Put away your smartphone, turn away from your computer, and mute any technology that might make noise. It's a good idea to permanently turn off most notifications on your phone anyway. Do you really need to know every time somebody likes your post on Facebook? Do you need to know the moment that someone shared your photo on Instagram? Probably not. The average adult checks their cell phone 110 times a day. That's a glance every thirteen minutes. Instead of trying to resist the urge to look at it while you're talking, just keep it out of sight.

Conversations require patience and focus, two qualities that are not easy to cultivate. I don't see that as a drawback, though—I think the challenge adds to a conversation's beauty. Conversations are precious because they require you to share time and focus equally with someone else instead of indulging your own thoughts. In doing so, you follow the natural flow of human interaction and allow yourself to be led into new, unfamiliar territory. You already know what's inside your own head; open yourself to the surprise and discovery inherent in someone else's perspective. It's worth the effort.

15

LISTEN!

The only reason why we ask other people how their weekend was is so we can tell them about our own weekend.

—CHUCK PALAHNIUK

In 2003, radio producer David Isay had an idea for an ambitious new project. It was an exciting idea, and one that soon gained international momentum. But it was not a new one.

I say this not to malign David but to draw attention to his inspiration for this project: the work of broadcasting legend Studs Terkel. When Terkel died at the age of ninety-six, he had held just about every job possible at a radio station—he'd played characters on radio soap operas, read the news, written ads, and even hosted his own show from Chicago, *The Studs Terkel Program*. He interviewed a dizzying number of significant people on that show, including Dorothy Parker, Martin Luther King Jr., Bob Dylan, and Tennessee Williams.

But it wasn't his celebrity interviews that won him a Pulitzer Prize. Terkel is best remembered for the conversations he had with quite average, historically unremarkable people. Terkel spent years gathering thousands of hours of oral histories. He traveled around the nation knocking on doors, hanging out in diners, and listening to people's stories. He talked to people who had lived through World War II and the Great Depression, asking them questions and then sitting quietly while they spoke, his tape recorder rolling.

One of his earlier books is called *Working: People Talk About What They Do All Day and How They Feel About What They Do*.[1] Not a very sexy title, and the characters in the book—a garbageman, a barber, a hotel clerk, a piano tuner, and dozens more—didn't have glamorous jobs. These were people you might pass at the grocery store without noticing, but whose stories were captivating and heart-wrenching and utterly unique to them and their lives. The book achieved global renown and even became the basis for a Broadway musical.

Terkel kept interviewing people and kept writing books. The archive of his work includes more than nine thousand hours of interviews with more than five thousand people. It's a treasure trove of history and humanity. The headline for his obituary in the *New York Times* described him as a "Listener to Americans."

Studs Terkel often credited a portion of his success to his childhood. He grew up in Chicago, where his parents ran a boardinghouse. All kinds of people would stay at the Terkel home, many of them immigrants, and young Studs would sit in the lobby and listen. He never lost his ability to listen and he never lost his passion for hearing people's stories. In his memoir he wrote, "What I bring to the interview is respect. The person recognizes that you respect them because you're listening. Because you're listening, they feel good about talking to you."

And that leads me back to David Isay. Decades after Studs Terkel sat listening to people in their kitchens and dining rooms, Isay thought it might be time to start listening again. He launched a project you may have heard of, called StoryCorps. The concept was simple. He installed a recording booth inside New York's Grand Central Terminal and invited people to come inside and have a conversation. There are now StoryCorps booths in Atlanta, Chicago, and San Francisco, along with a mobile booth that travels thousands of miles every year, collecting the stories of those who are willing to share.

StoryCorps has been incredibly successful. Isay and his colleagues have recorded tens of thousands of interviews and a select few are broadcast every Friday during NPR's *Morning Edition*. When I see someone crying while they're listening to the radio, I usually assume they're listening to StoryCorps.

The stories span a wide array of topics and include everything from professions of love to postwar trauma. Past recordings have included interviews with children asking their parents what they were like when they were young, siblings reunited after years spent apart, and soldiers describing the long, lonely nights of deployment.

StoryCorps doesn't attract a lot of celebrities, just regular, average folks. And participants aren't paid; people choose to sit in a booth and talk for forty minutes because they want to be heard and remembered. Isay says the act of listening has a profound impact. "It's about honoring another human being by simply listening to them," Isay says. "The joke, of course, is that I'm a terrible listener . . . I'm just so easily distracted by my phone or email. . . . But that's why StoryCorps is so important. It's about learning to listen, and giving the gift of listening at a time when we are all barraged with so much other noise. It's about shaking someone on the shoulder, and saying, 'Hey. Let's talk about what's really important to you.'"[2]

Isay's words resonate with me because he admits that he's not a great listener but recognizes the power of listening and is actively working to be better. I feel much the same way. I'm not the best listener, either, but I know this skill is crucial to every relationship I have, and I am on a mission to improve.

The truth is that almost everyone struggles to listen well. Very few of us listen actively. That is, not just hear, but also understand, respond, and remember. The inability to do that is not a character flaw so much as it is a human one. Listening doesn't come naturally to our species, it seems.

Anyone who's spent time with an infant will tell you that we're not born listening, we're born making noise. Listening is a skill you must practice with intent. Ralph Nichols was a pioneer in this research and was deservedly known as the "Father of Listening." In the 1950s, he conducted years of listening experiments, and in his book *Are You Listening?*, he wrote: "It can be stated, with practically no qualification, that people in general do not know how to listen. They have ears that hear very well, but seldom have acquired the necessary aural skills which would allow those ears to be used effectively for what is called *listening*."[3]

We are wired to talk. Talking is useful. It can bolster and even shape our identities. Scientists at Harvard recently found that talking about ourselves activates the pleasure centers in the brain. The researchers asked study participants to talk about themselves and their own opinions and then to talk about other people and their opinions, all while hooked up to a functional magnetic resonance imaging machine (fMRI). The researchers observed that parts of the mesolimbic dopamine system became active when the participants were talking about themselves. That's the same area in the brain that lights up in response to sex, cocaine, and sugar. You read that right—talking about yourself causes a similar pleasure in your head as having sex or eating a chocolate truffle.[4]

Even more fascinating, the participants in the study had no reason to believe that anyone was listening to them. For all they knew, they were simply talking to themselves. And yet, they still experienced great pleasure from talking about themselves, even when they thought they were talking to an empty room.

This seems to suggest that we are not very objective in measuring the success of our conversations. How many times have you walked away from a job interview and thought, *I nailed that*, only to be surprised later that you didn't get the job? There could be any number of reasons why you weren't hired, but one of them might be that you talked about yourself more than you listened. So you felt great, but the person on the other side of the desk didn't. If we judge the success of a conversation based on how we feel, it could be that we're led astray by the dopamine surge we get from talking about ourselves.

In another study, researchers offered participants different amounts of money to answer a variety of questions, with the amount changing based on which questions people chose to answer. They could opt to answer a question about themselves, about another person, or about a fact.

Repeatedly, people chose to accept lower pay in order to disclose information about themselves. They accepted, on average, 17 percent less money in exchange for talking about their feelings and ideas. From the report: "Just as monkeys are willing to forgo juice rewards to view dominant groupmates and college students are willing to give up money to view attractive members of the opposite sex, our participants were willing to forgo money to think and talk about themselves."[5]

Our desire to talk more than we listen prevents us from having great conversations. I find it ironic that the phrase "I hear you" is so often used these days as a way to communicate that we are paying attention to someone. For one thing, the act of hearing happens involuntarily and doesn't necessarily involve listening. But more important, the truth is that most of the time we aren't really listening at all. I was at the grocery store recently and told the cashier, "My reusable bags are buried in my cart. Give me a minute to get them out." She looked directly at me and said, "Okay, sure. I hear you," *while she was bagging my groceries in plastic bags*. I had to repeat myself twice more before she really *heard* me.

How many times has someone said to you, "You're not hearing me!" What they really mean, I think, is, "You're not listening." I've trained myself to stop talking as soon as I hear any version of that complaint. In almost every case, when someone has told me that they are not being heard, they've been right. I had stopped listening to them.

One of the best measures of successful listening is retention, yet we rarely connect our ability to remember what's said to how well we listened. The research on retention that I mentioned in Chapter Six was conducted in the 1950s. Researchers found that if we are listening casually to something we're told, we will forget up to half of it within eight hours.[6] Even if we're listening very closely and focusing intently, we'll forget 75 percent within a couple of months. Remember that active listening is defined as hearing, understanding, responding, and retaining. Yet, humans don't naturally listen that way, and haven't for decades.

*　　*　　*

It's quite possible that we were better at listening at some point in our history. With all of our recent technological advances, it's easy to forget that reading material has only been widely available for a few hundred years. For centuries, our primary source for information and education was the spoken word. Before the invention of the printing press, your education depended on your listening skills. It's only very recently that we began to find it a waste of time to listen to other people.

Unsurprisingly, the ways in which we consume information today are further damaging our listening skills. When we read online, the multitude of pictures and videos and links can overwhelm our minds, so our brains have learned how to skim.[7] Our eyes unconsciously look for keywords and bullet points. We gloss over details and nuance and go directly to what our brains perceive to be the crux of the material.

Researchers have learned that these habits are now following us off-line to the printed page. Getting through *War and Peace* is substantially more difficult for today's students than it was for their parents and grandparents. And we are no better at listening to someone at length than we are at reading a long article on the Web without clicking over to another tab to check our e-mail. We skim through our conversations.

If you are accustomed to people expressing themselves in 140 characters or fewer, it can be difficult to remain engaged while they spend ten minutes describing what happened to them at work. Even online, where the stories are enhanced by charts and graphs and cool fonts and pictures, many people don't read past the headlines.[8] Our brains struggle to focus for long on what someone else has written or is saying. This is something that neuroscientist Maryanne Wolf calls Twitter brain.

While few of us are good, active listeners, most of us are blissfully unaware of our incompetence. The company Accenture surveyed thousands of people in thirty different countries, evenly split by gender. Almost all of them said they were good listeners.[9] But the facts suggest they are probably deluded about that. Ninety-eight percent of those surveyed admitted they spend a good portion of their days distracted; more than half reported that working digitally interferes with their ability to listen; and 86 percent said they multitask during conference calls. Remember, humans are unable to multitask. There's no way you can listen well on a call if you're checking your e-mail or typing up a document at the same time. We don't realize all the daily habits that interfere with listening, so we may think we're good at it when we're really not.

Most of us acknowledge the importance of listening, but we rarely take any action to get better at it. When asked, the majority of businesspeople and academics say listening is one of the most important skills required of an effective professional. And yet, fewer than 2 percent of articles in business journals address the topic of active listening. The same thing is true in our schools. You can easily find a class on public speaking but rarely one on how to listen. That's unfortunate because, as it turns out, listening must be taught.

Recent research out of Australia suggests that active listening is a conscious act and has to be part of specific instruction.[10] In other words, students learn to listen better if they are aware that they're being taught to listen. They don't pick it up while learning other things such as math and history. The researchers were especially focused on facial expression and body language in communication, as they say both are essential to effective listening. "To 'hear' the listener must not only understand what is being said verbally," the report says, "but also the non-verbal communication that informs what is said."

The experiment seemed to have great success by using Open Space Technology—a method for conducting meetings in which there is a specific, focused task but no formal agenda—in order to limit the use of computers and increase face-to-face interaction. The students were given a task and then divided into groups in a large, open room. They were instructed to listen carefully, to respond thoughtfully, and to be prepared to sum up what was said at the end of the session. The researchers sought to answer the question "Can students' understanding of the task be enhanced by listening to others?" and the answer seems to be yes.

Listening requires energy and attention and involves more senses than just hearing. There are three kinds of information conveyed during a conversation: lingual (the meaning of the words being said), gestural (facial expressions, hand movements, posture), and tonal (how we say the words).

We're all aware that the mere meaning of our words is not enough to convey a message effectively. Many of us joke about needing a "sarcasm font" for e-mail and social media, so that other people know when we're kidding. We've all had e-mails come across as snarky or insulting when that wasn't the intention. To understand what someone else is telling us requires more than a printed word. Listening requires our whole bodies and our full attention.

But many of us don't commit that fully to a conversation. We approach an exchange as an opportunity to articulate our own needs and opinions, not to hear someone else's thoughts. "Most people do not listen with the intent to understand," says author Stephen Covey. "They listen with the intent to reply."[11] We talk to someone because we want to say something, not because we want to hear.

All too often, our conversations are like the worst kind of music concert. Imagine a violinist playing one piece of music while the pianist plays another. They can be friendly and watch each other and nod all they want, but the end result will be cacophony if they aren't on the same page of sheet music.

It's not easy to break the habit of simply waiting for someone to take a breath so that you can speak again, but it can be done. First, try to listen for ideas. While the other person is talking, think about the deeper meaning of their words and their thoughts. Watch their facial expressions and gestures. What are they really trying to say? You can ask questions like, "Does that mean that . . . ?" or "Are you saying that . . . ?" Perhaps they're hinting at something. What is it? Why are they telling that story at that moment? What's the big idea?

Also, think ahead to what they might be going to say next. To guess what's coming, you must pay attention to what's happening. This carries risk, as you might be tempted to make assumptions about what they're saying instead of predicting based on what they're actually telling you. Because it's condescending to finish the end of someone else's sentence or story, it's best you keep these guesses to yourself. The act of guessing, though, will keep you engaged.

This next piece of advice is especially important in our current political climate: evaluate the evidence instead of jumping to conclusions. That means, listen to the words they're actually saying instead of listening for certain words or names and making assumptions about what they mean.

We often make up our minds about people based on a few familiar terms they use. If someone says they support the Second Amendment, we often believe we know all we need to about them. We don't listen because we think we can predict everything they'll say. We have already decided what our opinions are on certain subjects and don't want to hear arguments for the opposing view.

It is highly unlikely that any human being has all of the same opinions as the talking head you heard on cable news; you must listen to someone in order to discover the nuances of his or her position. Instead of shutting down when someone offers an opinion with which you disagree, weigh the evidence. Think about what it might mean if they're right. Where did this person get his or her information? You can ask. For that matter, how did you get *your* information?

Respond to what they say, not to what you think they said or what you expected them to say. Don't say the same thing to them that you said to the last liberal/conservative you spoke to. Listen and respond to what they actually said. That means you might sometimes have to ask them to clarify their positions. It means you might not know what to say. Having questions about what you heard is a good indication that you're listening.

Last, try to summarize what you're hearing, but do it in your head. This is another way to put the extra words in your mind to good use. Review what the other person has said and rephrase it. You will immediately notice if you missed something or if you're not clear on a specific point. Then you can ask a good question such as, "How did you get from the post office to the school? I missed that part." Remember that active listening is not just about passively sitting there in toleration while someone else speaks. A robot could do that. Listening is work.

I heard a lot of opera as a child. My grandfather wrote eight operas. His music was played often in our home, as was music by Verdi and Puccini and Mozart. Many American kids know the bits of Wagner played in Bugs Bunny cartoons, but I heard the whole Ring Cycle on a regular basis. And I never liked it. I thought opera was boring.

As a college student, I had planned to study classical theater. But when I transferred schools midway through my freshman year, I discovered that the only scholarships available at my new school were for voice students. I had four days to prepare an art song and an operatic aria for the audition. I listened to a lot of opera in those four days. I don't even remember what I sang anymore, but I do know that by the time I performed in front of the faculty panel, I had fallen hard for opera.

What changed? After years of simply hearing operatic music, I finally listened to it. Prior to that week, I had relegated the melodies to the background of my mind, not even paying close attention on those occasions when I was seated in a concert hall with the lights down. I simply allowed the music to play while I thought about other things. When I finally listened, really listened, the music moved me in a powerful way. It was almost a spiritual experience, and that's not far from the experience I have sometimes when I truly listen to other people.

The thing about radio reporting is that your goal is to speak as little as possible. You're trying to keep your source talking and you know that you won't be able to use any portion of the recording that has your own voice on it. So, you get into the habit of asking short, direct questions and then shutting your mouth and listening as closely as possible.

Sometimes, the interviews that I thought would be deadly dull turned out to be the most fascinating. I did a story on the Purple Lilliput mussel in Michigan and could not get enough of the scientist who had dedicated his life to saving the tiny, plain mollusk. I've spent an inordinate amount of time hanging out at gas stations and interviewing people there. I've encountered a dizzying diversity of folks from different backgrounds and income levels, all on their way to someplace unique and all with their own particular wisdom to impart.

If you want to become smarter, listen more. If you want a stronger marriage, listen actively. And if you want better friendships, stop talking and listen. "The most basic of all human needs," said Dr. Ralph Nichols, who pioneered the study of listening, "is the need to understand and be understood. The best way to understand people is to listen to them." I can say without exaggeration that listening is the most important skill I've acquired in my life.

I've had to stop myself from filling this chapter with quotes, because there are a ridiculous number of smart, accomplished people who have articulated better than I can the reasons why listening is the most important skill a person can develop. But let me return to the words of my favorite interview guest, Salman Rushdie. In his book *Two Years Eight Months and Twenty-Eight Nights*, there is a genie character who works magic by listening. When I asked Rushdie about her, he said, "She can put an ear to your chest and learn exactly your heart's desire. . . . I think writers have to be good listeners. One of the things you have to be able to do as a writer is hear what people are really saying and be able to represent that. So yes, listening is great magic."[12]

16

SOMETIMES WE SHOULDN'T TALK

In order to understand the world, one has to turn
away from it on occasion.

—ALBERT CAMUS

In my house, I don't make a lot of phone calls. If we need
to talk to the cable company or make a doctor's appointment, I pass that task along to my son. By the time I get
home from work, talking has exhausted me and I need
silence for a few hours. I often don't have the energy to
be chatty with the customer service rep or the landscap-
ing guy. Rather than risk being rude, I delegate those
conversations to someone else. By the time I'm done
with dinner, I'm usually ready to listen actively and engage with people positively.

This experience is not unique to me; science supports
the idea that not all conversation is healthy or helpful.
In 2010, a group of researchers at the University of
Arizona equipped dozens of students with recording

devices so they could track their conversations. These students were then asked to assess their level of happiness. Those who said they were happy tended to be people who spent their time in the company of others. In fact, the happiest students spent 25 percent less time alone and 70 percent more time talking to other people compared to their less social peers.[1]

That's not a particularly surprising result; we already know that humans are social animals and that loneliness and isolation tend to make us unhappy. But there was one aspect of the study that was revelatory: not all conversation contributed to happiness.

The researchers found that the happiest students spent a third less time engaged in small talk and had about twice as many substantive conversations as the rest of the group. They concluded that "the happy life is social rather than solitary and conversationally deep rather than superficial."

Most of us endure a certain amount of small talk every day: you ask the waiter how his or her shift is going or you talk about the weather with someone sharing the elevator. Sometimes there is no escape from it—you can't always wiggle your way out of a desultory chat with your boss, for example—but on the whole, sometimes the best conversation strategy is to not talk at all.

If you don't have the energy or motivation to focus on another person, it's best to isolate yourself. That's how you avoid angry outbursts or saying things you don't really mean.

Small talk may be grating, but other conversations can be downright exhausting. I recently had to excuse myself when a colleague started describing her sister's troubled marriage. I don't know that colleague well and had never met her sister. She needed to give voice to her concerns and receive supportive energy in return, but I didn't have the energy to spare. I told her, "I'm so sorry for this situation. I'm sure it's stressful. I wish I had the time to talk about it, but I have a deadline to meet today." That was a better solution than to listen with half an ear and then say something vacuous like, "That's too bad. What a bummer." Much better to send her in search of a more dedicated listener.

A good conversation requires energy and focus—two commodities that are often in short supply. If you're unable to engage meaningfully, I would advise not engaging at all. Be honest, be polite, and walk away.

It's neither helpful nor productive to involve yourself in a discussion when you're tired or irritated and headachy. If you force yourself to talk when you don't want to, you won't be satisfied with your end of the conversation and you probably won't retain what was said on either side. You should never feel guilty for walking away from a conversation in which you're not able to mentally invest.

That might come as a relief to those who fall on the introverted side of the spectrum. As Susan Cain made popularly known in her book *Quiet: The Power of Introverts in a World That Can't Stop Talking*, introverts are partly defined by how they get their energy. Introverts recharge during their alone time; being around other people, and talking to other people, can be overwhelming and depleting for them.[2]

But it's not just introverts who benefit from solitude; a little peace and quiet is good for just about everyone. A study out of the University of Illinois found that when teenagers were alone for at least 25 percent of their time outside of classes, they earned higher grades and were less prone to depression. Head researcher Reed Larson said, "The paradox was that being alone was not a particularly happy state. But there seemed to be a kind of rebound effect. It's kind of like a bitter medicine." The teenagers didn't enjoy solitude, but they felt better after being isolated and those positive feelings lasted for at least a week.[3]

There is also a great deal of anecdotal and scientific evidence that solitude boosts creativity and deepens thought. Think of Thoreau's tiny cabin at Walden Pond or Marcel Proust in his spartan Paris apartment, the walls lined in cork to cut down on noise. Solitude can be a wonderful thing.

But creativity experts say innovation is the result of a delicate balance between solitude and collaboration. In other words, Steve Wozniak may have invented the personal computer while he was alone at home, but the idea was a result of his work with Steve Jobs and his conversations with the members of his computer group. It was inspiration based on conversation, followed by focused thought carried out in isolation.

Dr. Mihaly Csikszentmihalyi's research is seminal on this subject. He said that "creative people tend to be both extroverted and introverted." Even if you are not an inventor or artist, even if you are extroverted, research shows you reap benefits from regularly spending time alone.[4] One Harvard study even demonstrated that we are more capable of feeling empathy toward others after experiencing solitude.[5] Avoiding conversation from time to time can actually improve your relationships with others and make future conversations better.

Unfortunately, solitude is not something most of us seek on a regular basis. Most people don't like to be alone. A group of researchers at Harvard and the University of Virginia conducted eleven different studies and found that people, in general, don't like to be isolated.[6] In fact, "many preferred to administer electric shocks to themselves instead of being left alone with their thoughts." That aversion to loneliness can tempt you to engage in a conversation even when you don't want to. But that might be a bad choice.

Remember, it's about quality, not quantity. Talking all day will not make you a great conversationalist and constant chatter doesn't increase the value of the words—even Beethoven becomes background music if it's playing all the time. It would be rare indeed if you were able to have engrossing, engaging conversations every time someone said hello. You probably can't. So, if you need the time on the subway to be quiet so that you're in the right frame of mind to listen to your family when you get home, then be quiet. And feel good about it.

Even if you only have one conversation a day, it should inspire and enlighten you. Those are the kinds of conversations that will enrich your life and bring you a greater understanding of the people and world around you.

CONCLUSION

What you do today can improve all your tomorrows.
—RALPH MARSTON

I didn't set out in life to dedicate myself to conversation and I certainly never envisioned myself as a conversational evangelist. I've arrived at this place after years of observation and experience and research. All of which have led me to believe that conversation has the power to change the world.

That may sound hopelessly naive to some people, including my fellow journalists. We are, in general, a pretty cynical crew. We spend our days reporting on the ugliness of human nature: fraud, corruption, violence, war, disease. We have a skeptical view of politics because we're behind the scenes every day, watching the sausage being made.

But when a horrific event occurs, such as Hurricane Katrina or the earthquake in Haiti, it is also our job to find and feature the human element of the story. We have conversations with traumatized and sometimes victimized people, and try to distill large amounts of information down to a clear story that might help our audience empathize with those whose lives have been forever changed by tragedy.

I started working as a reporter in 1999. As the years have passed, I've noticed that conversations have deteriorated and people seem to be less inclined to seek out information from diverse sources. We no longer feel we understand each other, and therefore we don't trust each other.

Certainly the proliferation of technology in our lives, in our palms and pockets, has not helped, but I don't blame this problem on the popularity of smartphones. I don't blame it on social media, although many of us have been fooled into believing that digital connection is the same as conversation. And while cable network pundits who make their living by turning every nonissue into a political argument may further fuel our polarization, I don't blame the media, either.

Frankly, I don't blame anyone or anything for the disintegration of our conversations. There is no definitive cause, but there is only one solution—and that is to start talking. The collapse of conversation is damaging to us as a society and harmful to our shared humanity.

While I was writing this book, I consulted with experts

in many fields and read myriad studies. I took in a large amount of information that was surprising and enlightening, but there was one bit of research that has stuck with me more than any other: a study that showed empathy is declining rapidly among young people.

Empathy is very different from compassion. Compassion is the ability to say, "I feel for you." Empathy is the ability to say, "I feel with you." Compassion allows you to remain separate from the other person; it allows you to see them as "other." It can devolve into pity. Empathy forces you to feel connected to the other person and to recognize that we are all human, all struggling, all linked.

Doctors with empathy have healthier patients.[1] Empathetic managers have employees with higher morale who take fewer sick days. The ability to feel empathy is associated with less prejudice, less bullying, and more charitable acts. Empathy is also the basis for our morality. The Golden Rule is "Do unto others as you would have them do unto you," but you must have empathy to equate another person's needs to your own.

Scientists have identified many ways to foster empathy, including playing music in a band[2] or reading more novels,[3] but one of the most effective methods is conversation. Good conversation allows you to learn about someone else's experience, to compare it with your own and imagine how it must feel to walk in someone else's shoes. The researchers at the Greater Good Science Center at the University of California, Berkeley—an organization dedicated to using neuroscience and psychology to create a more resilient and compassionate society—recommend increasing empathy through interaction. They offer four simple ways to increase empathy:

1. Active listening
2. Sharing in other people's joy
3. Looking for commonalities with others
4. Paying attention to faces

Want to accomplish all of these things at once? Have a conversation.

The best conversations happen between two people who are considering each other. That's the definition of consideration, after all, to think carefully about the effect of what you say and do and try to avoid upsetting or harming another person with your words or actions. It's not always easy to do this—social scientists say narcissism is on the rise and it takes effort and practice for us to consider others.

CONCLUSION

Ultimately, the tools and strategies I've offered in this book share one underlying purpose—and that is to help you consider others when you're talking. Because doing that will make not only for better conversations but also for better relationships and, ultimately, I hope, a richer life.

Focusing on other people is good for more than just your conversation skills. We've known for years, for example, that volunteering can boost mental health. Donating your time to help others has been shown to reduce loneliness and symptoms of depression.

Helping others can make you happier, and recently scientists learned that doing charity work can even make you healthier.[4] One study showed that people who spend at least two hundred hours a year volunteering had a significantly lower risk of developing hypertension. Another study showed that people who volunteer regularly live longer.[5] So why doesn't everyone volunteer as preventative medicine? Here's the catch: these benefits were experienced only by people who *wanted* to volunteer, who enjoyed the act of it—not by those who volunteered simply because their job required a certain number of volunteer hours.

The same principle holds true for conversation. Your desire to know and understand others must be sincere or the benefits are greatly reduced. There is a significant difference between initiating a conversation with a colleague because you think having this person like you is good for your reputation, and initiating a conversation because you genuinely want to get to know him or her.

I wouldn't still be a journalist today if I didn't believe that access to information improves our society and that conversations build bridges between disparate communities. I believe with all my heart that we have a window of opportunity right now to make things better in our world. And it starts with an act as simple as saying hello to your neighbor.

So put away your smartphone for just a moment and go talk to someone. Better yet, go listen to someone. People will surprise you. They will delight you, enlighten you, and sometimes anger you. But if you can get past the superficial chitchat most of us mistake for conversation, people will never bore you.

Whenever your next conversation happens, I only hope it's a good one.

ACKNOWLEDGMENTS

There are many people to thank. On a macro level, every teacher I've had deserves thanks, as does every friend who's given me the blessing of their time and attention, and every guest that's consented to an interview.

On a micro level, let me express my gratitude to those who had the most direct impact: Julie Will, my patient and careful editor who understood from the beginning how important this issue is; Heather Jackson, the world's smartest and most supportive agent; Carol Kino, Theresa Bierer, and Beth Jones, great friends, smart women, and supportive ears; Don Smith, always willing to read and edit and give me an honest opinion; Teya Ryan and the staff at GPB; Pete Sandora, who helped me find my inner power and taught me to say no; Cynthia Sjoberg, who is basically Superwoman; Doug Mitchell, my bwana, who has been so honest and so supportive and so damn helpful, it's almost impossible to thank him thoroughly; Kathy Lohr and Roxanne Donovan, the brilliant women of my book group; Cindy Carpien, Laura Bertran, and

Jacob Conrad, who are the best editors and mentors a journalist could ask for.

My biggest thanks go to my son, Grant. For most of his life, it's been just the two of us, and I couldn't have asked for a smarter cohort with a better sense of humor or more brains. I just wish there were fewer puns.

A thank you to the brilliant minds who first got me thinking about listening: Dale Carnegie, Ralph Nichols, and Studs Terkel. And much gratitude to the illustrious researchers whose work was both a resource and an inspiration: Sara Konrath, Mark Pagel, Steve Levitt and Stephen Dubner, Daniel Kahneman, Dave Isay, and the good people at Pew Research and the Greater Good Science Center at UC Berkeley. And a special thanks to Sherry Turkle, who helped sound the alarm about conversational decline and so generously gave of her time to listen to me when we met at the TED Summit in Banff.

A big thank you to TED, an organization wholly focused on sharing ideas and inspiring conversation. And finally, thanks to NPR, PRI, and all of the dedicated journalists of public media. Public radio has fostered and informed great conversation since it was born more than a hundred years ago. It's also given me the opportunity to talk to some of the most creative, thoughtful, and interesting people in the world.

NOTES

INTRODUCTION

1. National Transportation Safety Board Bureau of Accidents, *Air Florida, Inc., Boeing 737–222, N62AF, Collision with 14th Street Bridge*, Aircraft Accident Report, Springfield, Virginia, National Technical Information Service, 1982.

2. Michelle Clark, "Study: Poor Communication Leads to Malpractice, Death," *Patient Safety & Quality Healthcare*, February 3, 2016.

3. France Neptune and Mallery Thurlow, "A Heart Wrenching Update from Haiti," interview by Celeste Headlee and John Hockenberry, January 13, 2010.

4. Wesley Morris, "Why Calls for a 'National Conversation' Are Futile," *New York Times*, August 2, 2016.

1: CONVERSATION IS A SURVIVAL SKILL

1. Joseph Stromberg, "Where Do Humans Really Rank on the Food Chain?" *Smithsonian*, December 2, 2013.

2. Quoted in Mark Pagel, "Why We Speak," *The Atlantic*, June 24, 2016.

3. Ibid.

4. Cognisco, "$37 Billion—US and UK Businesses Count the Cost of Employee Misunderstanding," Marketwire, June 18, 2008, http://www.marketwired.com/press-release/37-billion-us-and-uk-businesses-count-the-cost-of-employee-misunderstanding-870000.htm.

5. Willis Towers Watson, *2009/2010 Communication ROI Study Report: Capitalizing on Effective Communication*, 2010; originally published by Watson Wyatt Worldwide.

6. Daniel Kahneman, *Thinking, Fast and Slow* (New York: Farrar, Straus and Giroux, 2011).

7. R. Agarwal, D. Z. Sands, and J. D. Schneider, "Quantifying the Economic Impact of Communication Inefficiencies in U.S. Hospitals," *Journal of Healthcare Management* 55, no. 4 (2010): 265–81.

8. Heather Boushey and Sarah Jane Glynn, "There Are Significant Business Costs to Replacing Employees," Center for American Progress, November 16, 2012.

NOTES

9. John Doerr, "How Top Sales People Lead Sales," RAIN Group.

10. Neil Howe, "Why Millennials Are Texting More and Talking Less," *Forbes*, July 15, 2015.

11. Michael Chui, James Manyika, Jacques Bughin, Richard Dobbs, Charles Roxburgh, Hugo Sarrazin, Geoffrey Sands, and Magdalena Westergren, *The Social Economy: Unlocking Value and Productivity Through Social Technologies*, McKinsey Global Institute, July 2012.

12. Ross McCammon, "Why a Phone Call Is Better Than an Email (Usually)," *Entrepreneur*, November 5, 2014.

13. Common Sense Media, *Technology Addiction: Concern, Controversy, and Finding Balance*, 2016.

14. Paul Barnwell, "My Students Don't Know How to Have a Conversation," *Atlantic*, April 22, 2014.

15. Jonathan Haidt and Marc J. Hetherington, "Look How Far We've Come Apart," *New York Times*, September 17, 2012, https://campaignstops.blogs.nytimes.com/2012/09/17/look-how-far-weve-come-apart/.

16. Q, *Leading in a Pluralistic Society*, Q Research Brief, 2016.

17. Christopher Groskopf, "European Politics Is More Polarized Than Ever, and These Numbers Prove It," *Quartz.com*, March 30, 2016.

18. David W. Brady, "Sure, Congress Is Polarized. But Other Legislatures Are More So," *Washington Post*, February 17, 2014.

2: COMMUNICATION AND CONVERSATION ARE NOT THE SAME

1. The Radicati Group, *Email Statistics Report, 2015–2019*, March 2015.

2. Pew Research Center, *Global Digital Communication: Texting, Social Networking Popular Worldwide*, updated February 29, 2012.

3. Sara Konrath, Edward H. O'Brien, and Courtney Hsing, "Changes in Dispositional Empathy in American College Students over Time: A Meta-Analysis," *Personality and Social Psychology Review* 15, no. 2 (2011): 180–98.

4. Joe R. Feagin, Hernán Vera, and Pinar Batur, *White Racism* (New York: Routledge, 1995).

5. Abdullah Almaatouq, Laura Radaelli, Alex Pentland, and Erez Shmueli, "Are You Your Friends' Friend? Poor Perception of Friendship Ties Limits the Ability to Promote Behavioral Change," *PLoS One* 11, no. 3 (March 22, 2016): e0151588.

6. Quoted in Kate Murphy, "Do Your Friends Actually Like You?," *New York Times*, August 6, 2016.

7. Leon Watson, "Humans Have Shorter Attention Span Than Goldfish, Thanks to Smartphones," *Telegraph*, May 15, 2015.

8. Andrew K. Przybylski and Netta Weinstein, "Can You Connect with Me Now? How the Presence of Mobile Communication Technology Influences Face-to-Face Conversation Quality," *Journal of Social and Personal Relationships* 30, no. 3 (2012): 237–46.

9. Keith Hampton, Lee Rainie, Weixu Lu, Maria Dwyer, Inyoung Shin, and Kristen Purcell, *Social Media and the "Spiral of Silence,"* Pew Research Center, August 26, 2014.

3: YOU CAN'T OUTSMART A BAD CONVERSATION

1. David Dunning and Justin Kruger, "Unskilled and Unaware of It: How Difficulties in Recognizing One's Own Incompetence Lead to Inflated Self-Assessments," *Journal of Personality and Social Psychology* 77, no. 6 (1999): 1121–34.

2. David Mahl, "The Upside of Divorce," *Psychology Today*, March 1, 2000.

4: SET THE STAGE

1. Marianne LeVine, "Minorities Aren't Well Represented in Environmental Groups, Study Says," *Los Angeles Times*, July 28, 2014.

5: SOME CONVERSATIONS ARE HARDER THAN OTHERS

1. Maria Saporta, "Xernona Clayton," *Atlanta*, May 1, 2011.

2. Robert Mcg. Thomas Jr., "Calvin F. Craig, 64, Enigma in Klan and Civil Rights Work," *New York Times*, April 24, 1998.

3. Carolyn Y. Johnson, "Everyone Is Biased: Harvard Professor's Work Reveals We Barely Know Our Own Minds," Boston.com, February 5, 2013.

4. Annie Murphy Paul, "Where Bias Begins: The Truth About Stereotypes," *Psychology Today*, May 1, 1998.

5. Lin Edwards, "Study Demonstrates the Evolution of Stereotypes," Phys.org, https://phys.org/news/2012–09-evolution-stereotypes.html.

6. Vinson Cunningham, "Obama and the Collapse of Our Common American Language," *New Yorker*, July 13, 2016.

7. Q, *Leading in a Pluralistic Society*, Q Research Brief, 2016.

8. Patrick Phillips, *Blood at the Root: A Racial Cleansing in America* (New York: W. W. Norton, 2016).

9. Marie Guma-Diaz and Annette Gallagher, "Power of an Apology," University of Miami press release, July 14, 2014.

10. Michael McCullough, "Getting Revenge and Forgiveness," interview by Krista Tippett, *On Being*, May 24, 2012.

11. Beverly Engel, *The Power of Apology* (New York: J. Wiley, 2001).

12. BBC News, "Warsaw Jews Mark Uprising," April 20, 2003.

13. Kazimierz Moczarski, *Conversations with an Executioner* (Englewood Cliffs, NJ: Prentice-Hall, 1981).

6: BE THERE OR GO ELSEWHERE

1. Jon Hamilton, "Think You're Multitasking? Think Again," NPR *Morning Edition*, October 2, 2008.

2. Quoted ibid.

3. Daniel J. Levitin, "Why the Modern World Is Bad for Your Brain," *Guardian*, January 18, 2015.

4. Ibid.

5. M. G. Siegler, "I Will Check My Phone at Dinner and You Will Deal with It," *TechCrunch*, February 21, 2011.

6. Celeste Headlee, "Barenaked Ladies Meet Shakespeare," NPR *Morning Edition*, June 3, 2005.

7. Ralph G. Nichols and Leonard A. Stevens, "Listening to People," *Harvard Business Review* 35, no. 5 (September–October 1957): 85–92.

8. Brigid Schulte, "Harvard Neuroscientist: Meditation Not Only Reduces Stress, Here's How It Changes Your Brain," *Washington Post*, May 26, 2015.

7: IT'S NOT THE SAME!

1. Charles Derber, *The Pursuit of Attention: Power and Ego in Everyday Life*, 2nd ed. (New York: Oxford University Press, 2000).

2. R. I. M. Dunbar, Anna Marriott, and N. D. C. Duncan, "Human Conversational Behavior," *Human Nature* 8, no. 3 (1997): 231–46.

3. Bonnie Badenoch, *Being a Brain-Wise Therapist* (New York: W. W. Norton, 2008).

4. Judith Martens, "Covey #5: Seek First to Understand, Then to Be Understood," *Behavior Change, Covey Series, Social Psychology*, July 16, 2013.

5. Max-Planck-Gesellschaft, "I'm OK, You're Not OK," October 9, 2013.

6. Michael W. Kraus, Stéphane Côté, and Dacher Keltner, "Social Class, Contextualism, and Empathic Accuracy," *Psychological Science* 21, no. 11 (2010): 1716–23.

7. Stephanie Pappas, "To Read Others' Emotions, It Helps to Be Poor," *LiveScience*, November 16, 2010.

NOTES

8: GET OFF THE SOAPBOX

1. Fon Louise Gordon, "Carrie Lena Fambro Still Shepperson (1872–1927)," *Encyclopedia of Arkansas History and Culture*, 2008.

2. R. F. West, R. J. Meserve, and K. E. Stanovich, "Cognitive Sophistication Does Not Attenuate the Bias Blind Spot," *Journal of Personality and Social Psychology* 103, no. 3 (2012): 506–19.

3. David McRaney, *You Are Not So Smart* (New York: Gotham Books, 2011).

4. Alexios Mantzarlis, "Fact-Checking Doesn't 'Backfire,' New Study Suggests," *Poynter*, November 2, 2016.

5. From the "lost interview" of Steve Jobs, conducted by Robert X. Cringely and featured in the 1996 PBS special *Triumph of the Nerds*.

6. Michael Dimock, Jocelyn Kiley, Scott Keeter, and Carroll Doherty, *Political Polarization in the American Public: How Increasing Ideological Uniformity and Partisan Antipathy Affect Politics, Compromise and Everyday Life*, Pew Research Center, June 12, 2014.

7. Keith Hampton, Lee Rainie, Weixu Lu, Maria Dwyer, Inyoung Shin, and Kristen Purcell, *Social Media and the "Spiral of Silence,"* Pew Research Center, August 26, 2014.

8. M. Scott Peck, *The Road Less Traveled and Beyond: Spiritual Growth in an Age of Anxiety* (New York: Simon and Schuster, 1997).

9: KEEP IT SHORT

1. Ian Hardy, "Losing Focus: Why Tech Is Getting in the Way of Work," BBC News, May 8, 2015.

2. Maia Szalavitz, "The Key to a High IQ? Not Getting Distracted," *Time*, May 24, 2013.

3. Quoted in Lisa Earle McLeod, "The Real Reason So Many People Are Such Bad Communicators," *Huffington Post*, March 25, 2011.

10: NO REPEATS

1. Stephanie Castillo, "Repeat After Me: Repetition While Talking to Others Can Help Improve Your Memory," *Medical Daily*, October 7, 2015.

2. Zachariah M. Reagh and Michael A. Yassa, "Repetition Strengthens Target Recognition but Impairs Similar Lure Discrimination: Evidence for Trace Competition," *Learning and Memory* 21, no. 7 (2014): 342–46.

3. Quoted in Joseph Stromberg, "Re-reading Is Inefficient. Here Are 8 Tips for Studying Smarter," *Vox*, January 16, 2015.

4. Gary Wolf, "Want to Remember Everything You'll Ever Learn? Surrender to This Algorithm," *Wired*, April 21, 2008.

11: THAT'S A GREAT QUESTION

1. Robert B. Cialdini, *Influence: The Psychology of Persuasion*, rev. ed. (New York: Harper Business, 2006).

2. Quoted in Ross McCammon, "Why a Phone Call Is Better Than an Email (Usually)," *Entrepreneur*, November 5, 2014.

3. James Stephens, *Traditional Irish Fairy Tales* (New York: Dover Publications, 1996).

12: YOU CAN'T KNOW EVERYTHING

1. Sean Gregory, "Domino's New Recipe: (Brutal) Truth in Advertising," *Time*, May 5, 2011.

2. Quoted in Alina Tugend, "Why Is Asking for Help So Difficult?," *New York Times*, July 7, 2007.

3. Steven Levitt, interview by Stephen Dubner, "The Three Hardest Words in the English Language," *Freakonomics Radio*, podcast, May 15, 2014.

4. Allen Francis, *What Should Doctors Do When They Don't Know What to Do (blog)*, *Huffington Post*, updated August 24, 2013.

5. Stuart Foxman, "The Three Hardest Words," Doc Talk, College of Physicians and Surgeons of Ontario; originally published as "The Three Hardest Words—'I Don't Know,'" *Dialogue* 8, no. 1 (2012).

13: STAY OUT OF THE WEEDS

1. Quoted in Lydia Dishman, "The Science of Why We Talk Too Much (and How to Shut Up)," *Fast Company*, June 11, 2015.

14: TRAVEL TOGETHER

1. Craig Lambert, "Ideas Rain In," *Harvard* magazine, May–June 2004.

2. Matthew T. Gailliot, Roy F. Baumeister, C. Nathan DeWall, Jon K. Maner, E. Ashby Plant, Dianne M. Tice, Lauren E. Brewer, and Brandon J. Schmeichel, "Self-Control Relies on Glucose as a Limited Energy Source: Willpower Is More Than a Metaphor," *Journal of Personality and Social Psychology* 92, no. 2 (2007): 325–36.

3. Tanya Stivers, N. J. Enfield, Penelope Brown, Christina Englert, Makoto Hayashi, Trine Heinemann, Gertie Hoymann, Federico Rossano, Jan Peter de Ruiter, Kyung-Eun Yoon, and Stephen C. Levinson, "Universals and Cultural Variation in Turn-Taking in Conversation," *Proceedings of the National Academy of Sciences of the United States of America* 106, no. 26 (2009): 10587–92.

4. Zoltán Kollin, "Myth #1: People Read on the Web," *UX Myths*.

NOTES

5. Harald Weinreich, Hartmut Obendorf, Eelco Herder, and Matthias Mayer, "Not Quite the Average: An Empirical Study of Web Use," *ACM Transactions on the Web* 2, no. 1, article 5 (2008): 1–31.

6. Simon Moss, "Ventrolateral Prefrontal Cortex," *SICO Tests*, June 30, 2016.

15: LISTEN!

1. Studs Terkel, *Working: People Talk About What They Do All Day and How They Feel About What They Do* (New York: Pantheon Books, 1974).

2. David Isay, "How I Learned to Listen," *TED Blog*, March 4, 2015.

3. Ralph G. Nichols and Leonard A. Stevens, *Are You Listening?* (New York: McGraw-Hill, 1957).

4. Adrian F. Ward, "The Neuroscience of Everybody's Favorite Topic," *Scientific American*, July 16, 2013.

5. Diana I. Tamir and Jason P. Mitchell, "Disclosing Information About the Self Is Intrinsically Rewarding," *Proceedings of the National Academy of Sciences of the United States of America* 109, no. 21 (2012): 8038–43.

6. Ralph G. Nichols and Leonard A. Stevens, "Listening to People," *Harvard Business Review* 35, no. 5 (September–October 1957): 85–92.

7. Michael S. Rosenwald, "Serious Reading Takes a Hit from Online Scanning and Skimming, Researchers Say," *Washington Post*, April 6, 2014.

8. Farhad Manjoo, "You Won't Finish This Article: Why People Online Don't Read to the End," *Slate*, June 6, 2013.

9. Samantha Cole, "New Research Shows We're All Bad Listeners Who Think We Work Too Much," *Fast Company*, February 26, 2015.

10. Donella Caspersz and Ania Stasinska, "Can We Teach Effective Listening? An Exploratory Study," *Journal of University Teaching and Learning Practice* 12, no. 4 (2015): 12–16.

11. Stephen R. Covey, *The Seven Habits of Highly Effective People: Restoring the Character Ethic* (New York: Free Press, 1989).

12. Salmon Rushdie in an interview by Celeste Headlee on the show *On Second Thought* from GPB (Georgia Public Broadcasting), September 16, 2015.

16: SOMETIMES WE SHOULDN'T TALK

1. Matthias R. Mehl, Simine Vazire, Shannon E. Holleran, and C. Shelby Clark, "Eavesdropping on Happiness: Well-Being Is Related to Having Less Small Talk and More Substantive Conversations," *Psychological Science* 21, no. 4 (2010): 539–41.

NOTES

2. Susan Cain, *Quiet: The Power of Introverts in a World That Can't Stop Talking* (New York: Crown Publishers, 2012).

3. Leon Neyfakh, "The Power of Lonely," Boston.com, March 6, 2011.

4. Mihaly Csikszentmihalyi, *Creativity: Flow and the Psychology of Discovery and Invention* (New York: Harper Perennial, 2013).

5. Neyfakh, "The Power of Lonely."

6. Timothy D. Wilson, David A. Reinhard, Erin C. Westgate, Daniel T. Gilbert, Nicole Ellerbeck, Cheryl Hahn, Casey L. Brown, and Adi Shaked, "Just Think: The Challenges of the Disengaged Mind," *Science* 345, no. 6192 (2014): 75–77.

CONCLUSION

1. The definition of empathy from *Greater Good: The Science of a Meaningful Life*, http://greatergood.berkeley.edu/topic/empathy/definition.

2. Stacey Kennelly, "Does Playing Music Boost Kids' Empathy?," *Greater Good: The Science of a Meaningful Life*, June 8, 2012.

3. Keith Oatley, "Changing Our Minds," *Greater Good: The Science of a Meaningful Life*, December 1, 2008.

4. Rodlescia S. Sneed and Sheldon Cohen, "A Prospective Study of Volunteerism and Hypertension Risk in Older Adults," *Psychology and Aging* 28, no. 2 (2013): 578–86.

5. Sara Konrath, Andrea Fuhrel-Forbis, Alina Lou, and Stephanie Brown, "Motives for Volunteering Are Associated with Mortality Risk in Older Adults," *Health Psychology* 31, no. 1 (2012): 87–96.

ABOUT THE AUTHOR

Celeste Headlee is cohost of the national PBS television show *Retro Report*, and has been a journalist since 1999. She started her broadcasting career at Arizona Public Radio in Flagstaff, then moved to WDET in Detroit, before taking a job with NPR. For several years, she cohosted the daily news show *The Takeaway* from PRI and WNYC. After that, she worked as a sub host for a variety of NPR shows, including *Tell Me More*, *Talk of the Nation*, *Weekend Edition*, and *Weekend All Things Considered*. In 2012, she launched the daily news show *On Second Thought* from GPB in Atlanta.

In 2015, Celeste delivered a talk for TEDx Creative Coast in Savannah on how to have better conversations. The talk was featured on TED's website and now has millions of views.

Celeste's first book was *Heard Mentality*, designed to help those who want to start their own podcast or radio show. Celeste is also a classically trained soprano who performs whenever she gets the time. She lives in Marietta with her son and her two rescue dogs.